Why We
Fish

Robert U. Montgomery

Table of Contents

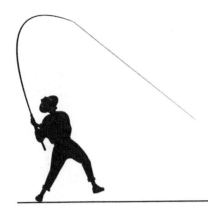

Introduction

*"Many men go fishing their entire lives
without knowing it is not fish they are after."*

—Henry David Thoreau

I like this quote from Thoreau because he simply, yet elegantly, extols the value of fishing. Yet it was written more than 150 years ago. In today's world, which is faster-moving and more complex than Thoreau's, many of us understand that fishing involves more than putting food on the table.

What is fishing all about?

With a little help from my fishing friends, including Bill Dance, I decided to answer that question in this book.

Let's not forget, however, that in the beginning we do go fishing to catch fish. It's that simple. And for a while, it's all about those fish. As young anglers, we're after numbers. As we age and gain experience, we want to catch bigger fish. And, eventually, we desire both.

For some, the yearning to catch fish lessens over time, especially for those fortunate enough to enjoy abundant success. For them, the "experience" of fishing begins to take priority. They take great pleasure just being on the water with family and friends.

That's not to say they no longer want to catch fish. That desire never goes away.

But whatever our motivation, no matter where we are on the success spectrum, fishing makes our lives better in ways we never could have imagined. It slows us down. It sets us free. It teaches us about nature, even as it reveals how much we don't know. And fishing is the foundation for many of our fondest memories.

This book examines the reasons we keep going back to the water and how that experience enriches us, both individually and as a society. The essays on these pages celebrate both the tangible and intangible blessings we derive from a pastime enjoyed by nearly 60 million Americans. (That many people say they've gone fishing within the past five years and consider themselves anglers. About 40 million buy fishing licenses annually.)

Some of these essays deal directly with why we fish in a world more complicated than Thoreau's. Others not so much. But they all are interconnected in the big picture of why we fish.

Author's note: I wrote most of the essays, but I didn't want my voice to be the only one in this book. That's why I asked nine others to contribute. They all share my passion for angling, and I'm proud to call them friends. I know you'll enjoy reading their insights into why we fish.

Robert Montgomery

In the Beginning . . .

*I*f fishing didn't save my life, it—at the very least—preserved my sanity.

For a year, it provided my only respite from thinking about the horrific way two of my best friends died. Being on or along the water with a rod in my hand kept me tethered to the simple but profound pleasure of angling, allowing my mind to escape the persistent mental visions of what their bedroom must have looked like in the wake of the murder/suicide.

Eventually, the nightmares stopped and I healed. Still, I will need a "maintenance" dose of fishing to bring me peace and joy for the rest of my life.

Why? Because fishing is good for me, a fact I learned long before my friends died.

Here's what happened:

As a child, I loved to fish. I lived to fish.

Then it wasn't about the "experience." It was bloodlust, pure and simple. I wanted to catch, kill, and eat anything willing to bite my bait.

From a little lake down the street, I brought home bluegills, green sunfish, bullhead catfish, and, once in awhile, a small bass. A neighbor showed me how to clean them. For a nine-year-old boy cleaning was fun too, especially poking around in the stomachs of the catfish, where I found crayfish claws, rocks, lead sinkers, and rusty hooks. I cherished the puncture wounds on my hands from spines and dorsal fins as much as I loved my favorite baseball cards.

My mother deep-fried the fish, and we ate them with corn bread, onions, French fries, and coleslaw. Few foods since have tasted so good.

Somewhere along the way, fishing evolved into something more for me.

A pivotal moment occurred during the spring of my sophomore year at college. Finals were coming up. Yearbook deadlines loomed. I needed to find a band for the spring formal. My seasonal part-time job had just started again. I had many tasks and little time to accomplish them, but I was young and strong. I could handle this.

As I walked outside following a student senate meeting, I began to shake. At first I felt perplexed. The day was warm and the air smelled sweet. The warm sun felt wonderful on my face, and yet the tremors intensified.

Then I began to cry. My chest grew tight and I gasped for breath. Friends walked me into the dean's office. He was kind and solicitous. As he guided me to lie down on a conference table and sent someone for a blanket, he asked if I was having problems with family or grades—or maybe a girl.

"No," I told him through my blubbering. "I don't know what's happening. Everything's great!"

The dean kept me there until I regained control. I was beyond embarrassed by my behavior as I climbed off the table and blew my nose a final time.

"You'd better see a doctor," he said.

I nodded, but first I had to do something else.

I climbed into my rusty Ford Falcon and headed out of town. As I drove, the tightness in my chest may have loosened, but I didn't notice. My eyes were on the road and my thoughts focused on the lake. I wanted to be there. I needed to be there.

The water was green and clear, with just a tinge of pollen floating on the surface. Squirrels made the only sounds as they scampered through leaf litter—and then they were gone. Feeding fish dimpled the surface in the little cove surrounded by oaks and pines and blooming dogwoods. Yes, the bass would be biting today, I told myself, as I popped the trunk to ready the tackle I always carried with me.

I tied on a purple worm rigged with a propeller harness and cast parallel to the bank as I walked along. Somewhere along the shore, my mind clicked into free spool and all the worries I'd been obsessing about drifted away with the current. I focused solely on the feel of the line between my fingers and anticipation of the strike.

And I did catch fish. The bloodlust had long passed, and I gently unhooked and released bass after bass.

I might have walked a mile. I might have walked ten, as I circled the small lake again and again. Finally, the first whippoorwill of evening broke the spell, and I realized I should be getting home for supper. My mother would be worried, especially if someone from the college called to tell her what happened.

I did go to the doctor the next day. Today, he would probably order a pharmaceutical to help me relax. In that more innocent—and no doubt healthier—time, he said I'd experienced an anxiety attack and should cut back on classes and activities. I dropped my 7:40 a.m. sociology class, even though I was acing it, and sleeping later three days a week did help.

But fishing is what saved me, of that I have no doubt. I didn't realize it at the time, at least consciously, but my subconscious knew.

In the years since, I've learned that fishing is an evolutionary trip that begins with a youthful quest to keep and eat, and it ends with... Well, I'm not sure where it ends, since I'm still enroute.

What I do know is that somewhere between age nine and nineteen, angling became a way to relax and empty my mind as surely as if I were sitting with crossed legs on a mountain in the Himalayas.

(Don't get me wrong; I still occasionally keep fish to eat. But long ago, harvesting fish became a side benefit to casting a line.)

Decades later, fishing for me remains a meditation. Yes, I still love catching—and releasing—fish. But nothing relaxes me and lowers my blood pressure like being on the water. For some reason I can't explain, the worry synapses stop firing in my brain when I hold a rod, and my hands take over. My mind snaps to respectful attention and is right there with the rest of me on that lakeshore or in that boat, living in the now.

As I've come to consciously recognize this blessing the Angling Gods bestowed upon me, I've also realized the key to happiness—even survival—in the increasingly hectic pace of modern life is to participate regularly in an activity that frees the mind and restores the soul. Angling was given to us by a higher power for exactly that reason.

If you fish, you know I'm right. If you don't understand, then go fishing—not just once, but a couple of times at least—and then you will know.

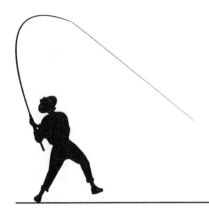

The Best Day

We say bad fishing days don't exist, but that isn't exactly true. What we really mean is, we never have bad days on the water, no matter how uncooperative the fish are.

Exploring exactly why bad fishing days don't exist is one reason I decided to write this book. For now, let's just say this: A bad day of fishing is an oxymoron, like "jumbo shrimp" and "living dead."

Some days, however, are superior to others, and one of the primary reasons is that fish *are* biting on a superior day. That day becomes even better when the bite is extraordinary. The best day of all happens when the bite is totally unanticipated. That thought leads me to my best day of fishing ever, because it was a combination of those two factors.

I've had a few other extraordinary days, including several on Mexico's Lake El Salto, as well as a couple in Canada and Costa Rica. Hopeful expectations accompanied those days on the water.

That certainly was *not* the case on this early summer day, angling for smallmouth bass out of Door County, Wisconsin. With several different guides who gave it their best, I had been trying to fish the Green Bay side of Lake Michigan for several days, but an unusually cold and brutal wind for June persisted out of the west, blowing right into our faces.

In short, we worked hard to avoid and/or navigate the rough waters and catch a few bass. Going into my last day, the trip had been most unmemorable in terms of angling success. Yes, I enjoyed seeing the bay and its scenic shoreline, meeting the guides, and learning new tactics, but I truly did want to experience some steady action before starting the long drive back to Missouri.

Capt. Dale Stroschein told me we would forgo another bayside attempt into the teeth of the wind and fish the main lake on the leeward side of the peninsula. Fewer protected areas were there, he explained, but he knew of a couple, and one in particular that might meet our needs.

We ended up in a small cove, opening to the main lake on the south. Fishing the upper end did, indeed, protect us from the wind, but the shallow waters didn't seem particularly promising. Most of it looked to be two or three feet, with a few spots a little deeper. Yes, I had caught smallmouth bass in skinny water before, but mostly while river and stream fishing.

Still, angling for a change in relatively calm water, with a warm sun on our shoulders, was a pleasant reprieve from previous days. We both threw spinnerbaits. At the ready, I also had light spinning gear rigged with a prototype coffee tube from Strike King, designed by my friend Troy Gibson. He came up with the idea when he threw the remains of his coffee, including a few grounds, into the water and was surprised to see how it attracted and excited bluegill.

Throwing toward a deeper hole, Dale connected on the second or third cast and fought a solid 4-pound smallmouth to the boat. Several other bass of equal size or larger darted to and fro around the hooked fish, which gave me the first inkling that maybe, just maybe, we would catch a few bass, but fish had misled me before; they are well known for that.

After netting my guide's bass, I picked up the spinning rod. "If you get some more excited fish near the boat, maybe I can tease one into biting the tube," I said.

He expressed doubts. "They don't usually bite when they're close like that," he said.

But one of them did this time. Dale hooked up on the very next cast. As he muscled the fish near us, I flipped the tube a few feet out.

Bam!

"Wow!" the guide said. "I've never seen that before."

Of course, my first thought was that Troy had created a magic bait and I was the beneficiary of its power. Even now, I think there might be some truth in that. The Lake Michigan smallies loved those coffee tubes that day.

They also hammered spinnerbaits and wallowed all over surface baits. They struck so hard on the former that they nearly pulled the rod from my hands a couple of times.

The setting—calm, shallow water—and the bite reminded me of fishing for cruising redfish in Louisiana or Florida.

The *smaller* ones were three pounds, and we weighed several that checked in at 5-1/2 pounds or more. Doubles were common, and we often caught three, four, or even five fish on successive casts. We didn't keep count, but we certainly caught more than 50 quality smallmouths in three to four hours of fishing.

Even for my veteran guide, the bite was extraordinary. He took a break from the action to call a friend and tell him about it.

As the bite finally slowed a bit, Dale wrestled a smallmouth that clobbered a topwater, while I battled another on a spinnerbait. When his fish neared the boat, I grabbed the net with one hand as I clung to my rod with the other.

His was a huge bass, possibly seven pounds or better, and definitely the biggest fish of the day. If it had been hooked on a spinnerbait, we might have landed it, but as the bass thrashed and tailwalked all over the surface, it was connected to Dale's line only with the tenuous treble of a topwater. When I reached out to stick the net under the fish, the frame touched it, sending the bronzeback into even more violent spasms.

In a heartbeat, then, it was gone.

On any other morning, I think losing a bass like that might have ruined our day, and, for me at least, it did create a slight blemish. I hate making a mistake when trying to net a friend's fish.

We both were thoroughly exhausted and exhilarated by the nearly non-stop action from fierce, broad-shouldered smallmouths that, for some reason, were stacked up in that small, shallow cove. A thunderstorm loomed on the horizon.

As we headed back to shore, I asked Dale why the smallmouth bass were there. He theorized that maybe they liked the cove because its water was too shallow to allow invasion by zebra mussels, which cover so much of the Great Lakes bottom in dense colonies.

Or maybe, like us, they were seeking a quiet place to spend the day away from the persistent west wind.

Whatever the reason, that day was my best ever, not just because the fishing was so extraordinary—and it was—but also because the experience was so unanticipated. On the water, you just can't get any better than that.

"It's the Same as Breathing"

*R*oss Gordon asked visitors to his Mystery Tackle Box Facebook page why they fish. He received several hundred responses. The following are some of my favorites:

- Makes a heroin addiction look like a craving for something salty.
- Why wouldn't you fish?
- Because fish don't talk back.
- It brings me peace of mind and is the best thing my dad ever taught me to do. When I fish I imagine he's right there with me.
- Relaxing one second and a pure rush the next.
- For the light before the sun comes up over the trees, the steam off the glassy water, the sound of my lure hitting the water, the early songs of the birds, the first strike of the day, and stories I will tell later that day and no one will believe. NOTHING is more relaxing.
- My brother and I used to fish a lot together. He passed away in 2009, and I fish to remember the love of fishing we shared.
- Because that is what the voices tell me to do.
- It's the same as breathing to me.
- To fish is to live with and appreciate nature.

- Because my wife won't go!
- Like many fly fishermen in western Montana where the summer days are almost Arctic in length, I often do not start fishing until the cool of the evening. Then in the Arctic half-light of the canyon, all existence fades to a being with my soul and memories and the sounds of the Big Blackfoot River and a four-count rhythm and the hope that a fish will rise. Eventually, all things merge into one, and a river runs through it. The river was cut by the world's great flood and runs over rocks from the basement of time. On some of those rocks are timeless raindrops. Under the rocks are the words, and some of the words are theirs. I am haunted by waters. (Although the person who posted this didn't say so, this quote is from Norman Maclean's book *A River Runs Through It*.)
- Do you need a reason?
- My granddad taught me to fish. Before he got too old and frail to get out there, that's all we did from when I was four years old to my early 20s. He still loves to hear my stories and see my fish pictures, and he turned 90 last week. I fish for the love of fishing, thanks to him!
- For those three seconds when you feel the fish get on.
- Had to think about this question . . . I fish to share the experience.
- To be out with creation and the creator.
- Because every time I get a fish hooked it feels like I'm 6 years old again! No matter how many times it happens.
- It provides an alternate means of therapy in a stress-free, non-medical environment
- Because of the MYSTERY!
- To find the real heaven.
- To study and learn.
- Fishing is the greatest thing in the world.

- Because I can't talk 'em into surrendering.
- Because when it's just you and that fish all your troubles just melt away. When you set the hook, you don't worry about your job, bills, social obligations, or any of that. It's just you and the fish.
- To have that rush of being scared. There is nothing like reeling in a HUGE musky. You get scared for a moment. Then you get down to business. Besides it's fun!
- Gave up golf for it. A LOT more relaxing and enjoyable and I can do it until I die.

According to a survey, more than two out of three fishermen
fish to spend time in the outdoors.

Occasions for Hope
By Dave Precht

(Dave Precht is vice-president of editorial and communications for B.A.S.S. He also is a great editor and good friend.)

Why do people fish? Like all philosophical discussions, we could argue this through tomorrow and probably never arrive at the truth, or even agreement.

We can list several reasons, each applicable to some people some of the time.

The Recreational Boating and Fishing Foundation wants to know the answers. In a noble effort to increase participation in fishing, RBFF commissioned outdoor sports researcher Rob Southwick to survey anglers last winter and find out why they fish. With the data, experts will tailor marketing campaigns that hit the right buttons and convince "lapsed anglers" to buy fishing licenses and return to the sport.

I wish them success. Without new recruits and renewed license holders, sportfishing could someday become marginalized and regulated out of existence.

Anglers in the survey were asked to select three reasons why they fish among a list of eight answers. By far the winner, with 67.8 percent of votes, was "I fish to spend time outdoors."

The others, in order, were "to get away from the stresses of everyday life" (49.4 percent), "for the excitement of the catch" (46.4); "to spend time with family" (44.9); "to spend time with friends" (30.2); "to provide food for the table" (17.4); and "to create memories" (12.9).

All are good answers, and I would certainly have to agree that spending time outdoors is one thing that feeds the fishing urge for me, but it's not the main reason.

Interestingly, similar questions have been asked of fishermen in the past. Over the last few decades, the American Sportfishing Association polled other groups of anglers, and their findings are a bit different.

In one of the latest surveys, respondents had to pick just one reason. Being "close to nature" ranked third with 13 percent, while relaxation and spending time with friends and family were first and second with 35 and 33 percent, respectively. Identical surveys in previous years yielded quite different results.

The message to me is that a person's motivation for fishing can change from day to day and year to year, depending on the vagaries of life. For similar reasons, a person can fall out of love with the sport one year, and become obsessed with it the following.

For centuries, thoughtful men have tried to explain why we fish.

Henry David Thoreau pointed out, "Many men go fishing all of their lives without knowing that it is not fish they are after." But he doesn't say what they *are* after.

President Herbert Hoover gave it a go with, "The reason for it all is that fishing is fun and good for the soul of man." He said this long after the Great Depression, which began during his presidency, but it would have been appropriate during the ordeal. As noted in a recent *B.A.S.S. Times*, fishing participation has gone up during the current Great Recession.

My favorite thought is from John Buchan, the Scottish author: "The charm of fishing is that it is the pursuit of what is elusive but attainable, a perpetual series of occasions for hope."

That is the reason I fish. It's an occasion for hope. I hope to catch a limit of bass, or to out-fish my buddies. To catch a 10-pounder. To not get skunked. The more elusive the goal, the more rewarding its attainment. Put another way, it's the challenge of catching bass that drives me and, I believe, most bass anglers.

A couple of years ago, our own www.bassmaster.com website posted a weekly poll — unscientific but interesting — which found that bass anglers have different motivations from many other fishermen. Relaxation, contact with nature, and camaraderie ranked at the bottom. Nearly half (48 percent) picked "the challenge," while another 22 percent checked "the competition."

Why I Fish, Part II

In the June *B.A.S.S. Times*, this space was devoted to what I jokingly referred to as a "philosophical discussion" on the topic, Why Do People Fish?

As philosophical discussions go, this one doesn't quite rank with "how can you prove you exist?" but I thought it might be an interesting way to explore a question that invites individual and ever-changing answers.

I reported on several surveys that asked people to select reasons they enjoy fishing. The studies found little agreement among those who responded, but some of the most-mentioned reasons included, "to spend time outdoors," "to get away from the stresses of life," "to spend time with family and friends," and "the thrill of the catch."

None of those registered in a poll of bass anglers, who mentioned "the challenge," and "competition."

Then I invited our readers to sound off, to share their reasons for fishing.

I guess I shouldn't be surprised that the first response came from a professional philosopher. Vincent A. LaZara, Ph.D., is a retired college professor in philosophy as well as a passionate fisherman who has written about fishing for an outdoors website. (He also wrote the book, *The Realist-Instrumentalist Controversy In Quantum Mechanics*, but I'll save that one for another discussion.)

I think you'll find his reflections on fishing interesting:

"As a professional philosopher, I have done much reading and given considerable thought to the question," he wrote. "My motive for going fishing varies with the situation. I might take a vacation to spend time fishing with my family; spend a weekend away with friends, fishing for camaraderie; take 'alone days' to commune with nature while at the end of a fishing rod; fish to grill a catch on a camping trip, etc. Your comment about the 'challenge of catching bass' being your driving force was insightful and is likely a common denominator to why fishing is my activity of choice in the situations noted.

"On a more primal level, I believe the sport of fishing is driven by the basic hunter-gatherer survival instinct that accounts for much of human behavior in general, from stamp collecting to bird watching, to spending the afternoon shopping at the mall."

I didn't ask about shopping at the mall, but I'm beginning to see the connection.

LaZara continued: "There are three stages to the hunter-gatherer process: anticipation, expectation, and gratification.

"In **anticipation** of going bass fishing, we prepare by doing things like reading fishing articles, acquiring the latest gear, researching fishing spots, and tracking weather patterns. Next, in **expectation** of catching bass, we apply our many skills as we walk the shores or motor around in our boats seeking to find a pattern and making the many casts required to do so. Eventually, catching bass provides **gratification** that reinforces our fishing behaviors, so the stages of the process become a repetitive cycle, i.e., we go fishing again and again."

Now, I understand why I'm driven to go fishing again and again. I thought for a while it was an obsession.

To explain her motivation, reader Eva Vandrei turned to a fishing philosopher of her own gender, Dame Juliana Berners, who wrote in the 15th Century: "And if the angler catches fish, surely then there is no happier man." That's it, Eva wrote: "Happiness."

On a more somber note, *Bassmaster* Editor James Hall mentioned a family connection with which many of us can identify:

"I fish because my father fished," he said. "When I think about the most precious times I spent with my dad, we were surrounded by water. The lessons he taught me during those moments were oftentimes disassociated with the task at hand—girls, finances, religion, alcohol, politics—and sometimes for good measure he'd throw in a lesson on setting the hook.

"Cancer took my father away from me prematurely. However, without fail, I think of him when water surrounds me."

Good enough reasons, all.

Steve Honeycutt wore this shirt during the final celebration of his life.

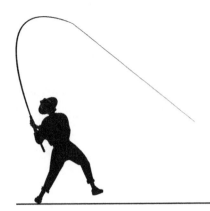

Everyday Hero

To say that fishing helped Steve Honeycutt live longer would be presumptuous, but it certainly made him happy and, more importantly, helped him endure. His body failed, but his spirit never bowed to the fatal cancer that took his life too soon.

Steve fished until the end of this life—and then some. Instead of a suit, the long-time tournament angler chose a tee shirt with an angler on the front and the message "Afterlife is Great! Simple as That" to wear at the final celebration of his life in Lexington, N.C.

His wife Kay, who agreed to bass fishing at Lake Norman on their honeymoon years earlier, remembered he made the decision to wear that shirt following a biopsy at the hospital. "After he told me, I looked at him like maybe he was still under the effects of medication," she recalled. "But then I knew he was serious." After all, she'd already made him a hat to wear and throw in the air after his "graduation" from radiation treatment. When chemotherapy took his hair, she saw him pose for goofy photos with his sons, who had shaved their heads in loving solidarity.

She was with Steve when he climbed Georgia's Stone Mountain just a month before his passing. In an e-mail update Steve sent to friends, he said of the trip, "I tell you, that was a proud moment for me. It was one of the hardest things I ever attempted (considering my physical shape). I declared I wouldn't do it again, but I may already be having second thoughts."

Steven Curtis Honeycutt, age 50, father of three, and member of the Archdale Bass Club, was just a guy who lived an ordinary life—in an extraordinary way. According to long-time friend Bill Frazier, who spoke at the celebration, during Steven's eight-month battle with cancer, everyone he knew, everyone he met, was inspired by his unassuming heroism,

"I know Steve," he told the gathering. "He does not want us grieving. He's wandering around the dock up there, worrying the snot out of someone about what hot lure the fish are biting and where he can get one.

"He's negotiating with old Saint Pete about how much tackle he'll be allowed to take on his next fishing trip with the Master Fisherman."

Frazier also said Steve was one of his "everyday heroes."

"Some people idolize comic book fantasies or sports icons," he explained. "The heroes in my life have always been there every day. They aren't necessarily close to me, but they are real. You can hear them, see them, and they see you.

"They are family and friends who laugh and cry, lead by example, struggle, and smile as they stumble along like the rest of us, slaying the common, everyday dragons we all face. But these people are special because they make it look easy.

"Steve became one of my everyday heroes long ago. We were fishing buddies."

Before he left the lakes on this plane of existence for those on the next, Steve logged in as much time on the water as he could, competing in two events. At his club tournament he could muster only enough strength to fish half the day, but of his participation at the North Carolina B.A.S.S. Regional less than a week later and less than two months before he died, he said, "I was able to fish the entire two days. God gave me that much more energy and stamina in just six days. I'm so blessed I can barely stand it! I didn't finish well, but I had a great time."

On the final day, a teammate saw him sitting away from the crowd, staring out at the water. Concerned, he went over and asked Steve if he was all right. "Yeah, man," Steve said. "It's the greatest day of my life."

Frazier explained such a description did not diminish the importance of family and friends for Steve. "To Steve, fishing was a reminder of who he was—unselfish but competitive, flexible but strong, beaten down but never a quitter. He was a warrior, courageous and unconquerable."

Back in April, after being treated with chemotherapy and radiation for esophageal and stomach cancer, he decided serving as a marshal at the Elite Series Blue Ridge Brawl bass tournament was more important than going to his doctor to find out the results of more biopsies.

The tests confirmed the disease had spread to his liver, but Steve was unbowed. He stayed at the B.A.S.S. tournament to fulfill his obligation as a marshal and spend time in a boat with some of the world's best bass anglers.

Steve was a big supporter of B.A.S.S., Frazier added. "Not the fish. The organization. For him, having just a regular old membership was the same thing as being in the NFL. He may have been irritated about one policy or another, but he never stopped supporting what he thought was the greatest bass fishing organization in the world."

Frazier, Steve's wife Kay, and many more of us whose lives Steve touched, wouldn't be surprised to learn he started a B.A.S.S. chapter and is staging bass tournaments with his afterlife fishing friends.

Sometimes a slow retrieve is better than a fast one.

Speed Trap ... Slow Down

*F*ourteen-year-old Jason and I were winter-fishing on Bull Shoals with my good friend Norm Klayman. I'm a Big Brother to Jason, who accompanies me on fishing trips as a reward for good grades.

We were throwing suspending jerkbaits. To be effective with this lure, an angler must jerk, jerk, jerk, and then pause, allowing the bait to sit suspended for a few seconds.

The bite usually comes when the lure is still. That's because a stationary bait makes an easier meal for bass and walleye, slowed by their cold-blood metabolisms in the icy water.

On this day, Norm and I eventually discovered the pause must be even longer than usual, because the fish were especially lethargic. We slowed down, and the two of us caught fish.

"They're not biting mine," Jason complained.

I'd been watching him fish. His retrieve was too fast and he didn't stop the bait. "You have to slow down," I said and turned my attention to my own fishing.

A few minutes later, I looked back, and he hadn't slowed. He didn't pause. If anything, he was fishing faster. Cast and reel. Cast and reel.

Jason didn't catch a single fish that day, just as he doesn't on others when a slow retrieve is required. Both Norm and I work with him, explaining how and why fast fishing isn't always good, but it doesn't take. Whether he's throwing a crankbait or a plastic worm, Jason insists on getting it back to the boat as quickly as possible so he can throw it again.

Even when we're fishing with nightcrawlers for catfish, he won't allow his bait to sit on bottom for more than a minute or two, even though I've explained these fish feed by scent and need time to find the bait.

As with our society in general, he feels the need for speed and desires immediate gratification, not realizing—or not caring—that sometimes slower is a wiser course of action, and sometimes just being on the water with a rod in your hand is its own reward.

Possibly if he fishes with me long enough, Jason will learn those lessons, but I am up against powerful opposition.

* * * *

Soft mist rises off the tumbling water, which makes the only sound in this idyllic setting. Against a background of giant spruce and snow-capped mountains, an angler expertly mends his line so a dry fly will drift toward a feeding trout. Yes, it is a place and time to be devoutly cherished, a dream image snatched from the minds of many fishermen.

Suddenly a metallic ring shatters the silence. The angler places his rod under his arm, no longer caring if the trout takes or what will happen if it does. He pulls a mobile phone from his vest, talks and listens for about 15 seconds, and then plops the phone back into a pocket.

"That's one that didn't get away!" he says with great satisfaction as he smiles toward the camera.

When I first saw that television commercial, I was angry. It took one of the most valuable reasons to be on the water—serenity—and dismissed it in favor of immediate gratification.

My anger quickly turned to sadness as I realized the commercial was merely a symptom of our society's mindless worship of speed and convenience, with the Madison Avenue advertising agencies as the high priests who lead us.

Truth be told, they don't care about us. They want us to buy stuff, and they lure us in by pitching their products as a way to improve our lives by saving time and effort. They beckon to us with faster food, faster weight-loss, faster-acting drugs, and faster internet-speed. They seduce us by promising "no waiting for loan approval." They woo us with labor-saving devices that provide "quicker cleanup."

Yes, sometimes "faster and more convenient" are better. Who doesn't want to download and upload faster on the Web? Who doesn't want faster relief from pain?

But just as bigger isn't always better, neither are quicker and easier. The person who spent years gaining that weight is putting his health, and possibly his life, at risk with diet pills. Just because you can get that instant loan doesn't mean you should. Too often, we fail to differentiate between what truly benefits us and what is a "deal" offered by the sirens of advertising in hopes we will buy their products.

This blind worship at the altar of speed bleeds into every aspect of our lives, especially for our children. Because we've learned we don't have to wait, we dart recklessly in and out of traffic, cutting in front of other cars so we can launch from a stoplight one second before they do. We have no patience for waiting in lines, common courtesy, or even listening.

That's why the attention span of students grows progressively shorter. That's why movies must contain explosions, car chases, and gun battles if they expect to succeed at the box office. That's why print media are on the decline, and that's also why participation in fishing flattened in some states and declined in others during the first decade of the 21st century. Actually "wait" for a fish to bite? No thank you!

Tournament angling has helped keep the sport vital, through its emphasis on faster boats and the need to cover as much water as possible during the hours of competition. Anglers "burn" spinnerbaits. Tackle innovators create reels with higher and higher gear ratios to speed retrieves even more. ESPN and other cable networks glamorize fishing events with helicopter coverage and heart-pounding music.

Am I a tournament angler? No, I am not. Competitors must put their fish in the boat as quickly and efficiently as possible. I like to play with mine, to watch them jump and tail-walk and, yes, sometimes throw the bait. If anything, I am the un-tournament angler.

I certainly do recognize the many contributions tournament fishermen have made to the sport, ranging from boat and tackle innovations to creation of a vocal constituency that finances and promotes conservation of our natural resources. I am an ardent supporter of fishing tournaments and happy to share the water with them.

Still, I believe faster is not always the best way in fishing, and from that I've learned it isn't always the best way in life either. Those who don't see that miss out on the many pleasures of the journey, as they focus single-mindedly on the destination. We each have only a limited amount of time in this life. Why rush it?

* * * *

Pro angler Kevin Short and I were fishing on Arkansas' Lake Greeson. We needed a "photo" fish for an article I was writing for *Bassmaster Magazine*. We managed a few fish early on topwaters, but they were too small. Faster-moving crankbaits totally failed. By late morning, we were dragging plastic worms, hoping a two- or three-pound bass wouldn't be able to resist such an easy meal, but no matter how much we slowed our retrieves, the bass just wouldn't bite.

Lulled into carelessness by the lack of action, I thoughtlessly tossed my worm right into the teeth of the wind. The bait flew out about ten yards and was stopped abruptly by the breeze. Loose coils of line spilled out of my reel in a large, cascading backlash.

"Oh, man!" I said. "This is going to take a while." I sat down and began picking and pulling. Fortunately, the mess wasn't as bad as I feared. About two minutes later, I was spooling the once-tangled monofilament back onto my reel.

As I tightened the line, I felt weight on the end. I set the hook and a three-pound bass catapulted from the water, my bait dangling from its jaw. It bit while the bait lay motionless on the bottom, a situation that never would have occurred if not for the backlash.

We had our photo fish, thanks to an ill wind that reminded me of the value of slowing down.

Through their field work, fishery biologists help maintain quality fisheries.

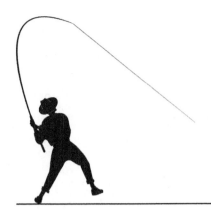

A Real Shocker

When I became conservation writer for B.A.S.S., the first thing I learned is that fishery biologists are an angler's best friends. In 25 years, I haven't changed my mind. They are *the* source for information about bass behavior and biology, as well as fisheries management. Their field work enables the states to maintain quality fisheries. Without them, chances are many of us wouldn't be fishing.

Electrofishing is one of the most important—and least understood—aspects of the biologists' field work. Want to learn what electrofishing is all about and how it helps you catch more fish? Ride along.

Rules vary from state to state, but in many states an angler can volunteer to go along on an electrofishing survey. This is one of several ways to get to know our best friends. You can also volunteer to help with cleanups, putting out fish attractors, and planting aquatic vegetation. You might enjoy assisting with events for children sponsored by your state wildlife agency or helping out in the booth during a weekend outdoor show.

"We encourage people to become involved," Florida biologist Bill Pouder told me.

You'd rather just fish? No problem. You still can learn what the biologists are discovering during their electrofishing surveys.

Oklahoma biologist Gene Gilliland suggests following along behind at a safe distance. "Watch what the biologists turn up and make note of the habitat each fish comes from," he continues. "When they stop to work up the catch, ask them to show you what they're collecting and fill you in on the latest survey results. It might surprise you to see what you've been missing." Gilliland says electrofishing is fast, efficient, and non-lethal.

"It allows us to catch large numbers of fish for length, weight, growth, and diet information," adds Georgia's Jim Hakala. "It allows us to see how well the fish are growing, weak and strong year classes, average fish size, how robust the population is, and, often, at what size anglers begin to pick up the harvest on a certain bass species."

What might you learn by riding along on a survey or talking to a fisheries biologist about his work? Sometimes you uncover something that will help you during a specific season:

Hakala once found frogs in the bellies of largemouth bass in February. "I figured the frogs they were eating were starting to emerge from the mud on the lake bottom," he theorizes. "As they stirred, they became easy prey for the largemouths. So the potential for an angler to throw a sinking frog imitation and be successful in February, when frog patterns aren't on an angler's mind, was potentially identified by the diet study."

Other valuable information is timeless:

"There are many times more bass out there than you could ever imagine," says Gilliland. He explains that an electrofishing boat often makes a pass down a shoreline and then a does a second pass, collecting fish that were missed the first time.

"I guarantee if I can't shock them all in one pass, you can't catch them all in one pass either," he says. "If you catch a bass, fish the same area again. That fish was there for a reason. "Something attracted it to that area and, chances are, more bass in the same vicinity were attracted for the same reasons."

The same strategy, he adds, should apply to a single piece of cover. Many likely looking stumps, bushes, and laydowns will yield no fish to the shocker, but one, for no apparent reason, might give up four or five bass.

"If you catch a bass, then fish that cover thoroughly and make it a point to visit the spot again later in the day."

Fish in thick cover, he adds, often have food in their stomachs. He believes that's because they've been out foraging and have returned to a safe place to digest their meals. Bass in open areas, however, often have empty bellies "because they're actively searching for that next meal."

To profit from this electrifying insight, throw a fast-moving bait between clumps of weeds and brush, especially during peak feeding periods of dawn and dusk, Gilliland advises.

"On the other hand, trying to entice a bass that has a full belly out of his hiding spot may take a great deal more patience," the Oklahoma biologist says. "Choose your lures and presentation accordingly."

Just what are the contents of those full bellies? When Georgia guide Mike Bucca rode along with Hakala, he was startled to see the forked tails of large gizzard shad sticking out of the throats of 4- and 5-pound spotted bass.

"That's likely why swimbaits perform well on big fish. A big fish has the means to routinely eat something large, but doesn't bite until that large prey is in distress. Then it pounces," the biologist says.

Hakala adds that he is more often surprised by how small the forage is. "I think a lot of times they (bass) select a certain size prey that's usually much smaller than what they can handle," he says.

But whether you're riding in a shock boat, cleaning up a shoreline, planting vegetation, or dropping attractors, the most valuable thing about volunteering is getting to know your best friends.

Bill Dance was a pioneer in using television to popularize fishing.
Photo courtesy of Bill Dance.

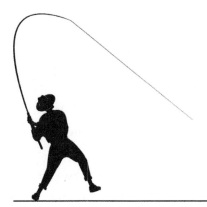

And Now a Word
From Bill Dance

(As one of world's best known and most beloved anglers, Bill Dance began his television career in 1968 on an ABC affiliate in Memphis. He was B.A.S.S. Angler of the Year three times during the 1970s, and is a member of the International Game Fish Association's Hall of Fame. He is also a good friend.)

I've often said there's a lot more to a fishing trip than catching fish. Just being able to go out there is something mighty special, but what are some of the reasons we go fishing?

I think that's a question you need to ask yourself. Fishing means different things to different folks. For me, fishing is my profession, but it's a profession I dearly love. What I'm saying is that I'm crazy about my job—and let me tell you why. Maybe some of my reasons are why you fish too.

First, it affords me the opportunity to get out into the great outdoors and lets me unwind from other pressures in life. It allows me to relax, be myself, have fun, and be competitive in an exciting way. It provides a perfect setting to be alone, or for togetherness with family or friends, whichever suits my mood. Fishing gives me a feeling of accomplishment. It teaches me patience, perseverance, and how to work toward goals. Hey, this is the only life I know and it gives me a great deal of pleasure to share it with you each week, as I have for the past 46 years.

Another reason we fish is because the human race is a competitive breed. We love to compete whether it's playing sports, going against each other on a field, watching a game on TV, or betting each other a six pack that an athlete will make or miss the field goal, the putt, the strike, the goal, the serve, and so on.

In sales, we compete to hit the $1,000,000 Club in insurance or the Top Car Salesman of the Month, and we play mental games with ourselves driving to work. We made seven traffic lights today; let's see if we can make ten tomorrow.

Fishing is no different, whether we're competing in a national bass tournament and fishing against 200 top bass anglers, or just spending a day on the lake by ourselves in a contest, one-on-one against one of Mother Nature's creatures that can be so unpredictable.

Finally the challenge to lure a fish out of his world into ours, with so many other competing elements, makes this sport special and is one more reason why we fish!

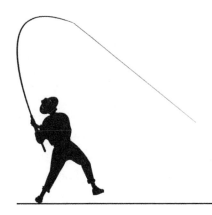

The Big Picture

*A*spiration is a big part of what makes us human. For fishermen, that translates into the desire to catch a big one. Size, of course, is relevant. I can get as excited about a one-pound bluegill as I can a ten-pound bass or a 100-pound tarpon, but here's the bottom line: that possibility of catching a big one is an important part of why I fish.

Awhile back, I went fishing for white sturgeon on the Columbia River, accompanied by my good friend Bruce Holt of G. Loomis, and golfing great Johnny Miller. Guide John Garrett put us on plenty of fish and I had an experience I'll never forget.

Seeing that first 10-foot sturgeon emerge from the depths at the end of my line had to be the highlight. Yes, the fight with a 500-pound fish was memorable, but visual confirmation of its incredible size made my knees buckle and inspired exclamations I rarely use.

It was a sight I'll always remember.

In five hours, we caught five sturgeon from 9 to 10 feet long, weighing between 350 and 525 pounds. We could have caught more, but wind and high waves finally chased us off the river.

With the three of us battered and beaten by the huge fish and the rough conditions, Miller asked the guide: "Have you ever killed a fisherman out here?"

"Not yet," said Garrett. "Not yet."

* * * *

Sometimes, the "big one" gets away, and that only intensifies the aspiration. Ask Bill Dance.

He would become one of the world's most famous and successful bass anglers from the late 1960s through the 1970s, and then one of fishing's most popular television personalities. But before that . . .

He was a young man, just married, that day on Pickwick Lake. He used a paddle to maneuver his johnboat down the side of a bluff, where hungry smallmouth bass chased shad.

"I had just missed a 2-1/2- to 3-pounder," he recalls. "It had rained a lot and I was looking at a waterfall on down the bluff. When I looked back down at the lake, my little old popper just disappeared. I thought it was a bluegill, at first."

Instead, it was a bass Bill Dance will never forget.

"He jumped five times," the Tennessee angler says. "I saw four of them. The other time, he ran under the boat and jumped behind me before I even knew what happened. I saw him four times in the water and four times out of the water. My Uncle Ben used to smoke cigars. He looked like a walrus with one tusk because you could see about an inch and a half of the cigar sticking out of his mouth.

"When I saw that orange popper sticking out of the fish's mouth, I thought of Uncle Ben. I could see just a little of that popper. The rest was in the fish's mouth, including two sets of treble hooks."

With the fish so well hooked, Dance understandably thought he was about to land the biggest smallmouth bass of his young life, possibly even a world's record. Based on mounts he'd seen at a taxidermist's, he was certain this bass weighed more than ten pounds, but the next time the bass ran under the boat, the line went slack, and Dance retrieved his fishless popper.

He was devastated.

"I wanted to catch him so bad," he remembers. "I went back there for weeks and months. I went back early and late. I went back at night. I fished up and down that bluff, knowing smallmouth bass have home-range tendencies. I went for a year, I know."

And he spoke often of the one that got away.

Finally, wife Diane said, "I know what that fish means to you. It will be imprinted on your mind for the rest of your life. I know how you feel and I'm so sorry, but will you please stop talking about that fish?"

Decades later, though, he still talks.

"People ask me about the biggest smallmouth I've ever caught, and I'll say three 8s," Dance says, "but then I'll add, 'Let me tell you about another one.'"

Pro or amateur, young or old, all of us who fish have hooked fish that got away. Fortunately for our mental health, we don't remember all of them, but one or two stay with us always. Heads shaking, they leap majestically in our dreams and memories. They burn drag. They burrow into brush. They throw baits back at us, and splash us back into reality with a slap of their broad tails.

Often, as with Dance, we believe those lost fish are the largest we've ever hooked.

Such was the case for pro angler Kathy Magers the day she practiced for a tournament on Lake Fork, a fishery noted for its big fish.

"Esmerelda—as I later named her—was a huge bass that hit my lure like a small one," Magers says, "but when she came to the surface and saw me, I screamed with excitement and she screamed with fright! Finally, when she jumped, we knew she was about a 15-pounder. My heart pounded like a big drum."

Esmerelda followed the leap with a dive.

"I pulled too hard and my line broke," Magers says sadly. "So did my heart. I had lost the fish of my dreams."

The veteran angler blames herself for the escape. She had been in a hurry to get on the water that day, and neglected to replace old, frayed line with new.

"Shame on me," she says. "I didn't prepare well and I paid the price. Mistakes teach us life lessons, and I learned a valuable one. I will never fish again without having good line.

"Surely, Esmerelda lives and the next time I hook her, she'll be mine—if only for a quick photo before I release her. Now, I'm prepared."

Dave Burkhardt was prepared one fall day, fishing out of Anglers Inn on Mexico's Lake El Salto. He used newly spooled 20-pound line manufactured by his own Triple Fish line company. Also, the Florida angler had plenty of experience with big bass, having boated two that weighed more than 15 pounds each and another that topped 13.

"That 15-2 was in a submerged orchard," he remembers, "but I still was able to get it out of the trees. I still had some control."

This time, though, was different when he set the hook into a big fish.

"This fish was totally out of control," Burkhardt says. "It did what it wanted. I had the drag tightened all the way down and it just kept on pulling line."

As the bass pulled, Burkhardt kept saying, "It can't do that. It can't do that."

Yet it did.

As with the 15-2, this one, too, hit near standing timber. When it sped toward open water, the Florida angler dared to hope he might finally conquer this still unseen monster of a bass.

"I thought I was home free," he says, "but it kept going and going. Finally, it just broke off. The thing I'll never forget is my feeling of helplessness, even when it was clear (of the trees). I never gained a thing on that fish. It could have been a 20-pounder. The big two zero."

Sometimes, though, the fish we remember most aren't necessarily the biggest. Maybe we didn't even hook it. Such is the case for Chris Gulstad, executive director of marketing for PRADCO.

As a teen-ager, he was wading Minnesota's Elk River with friends one warm June day.

"On this particular day, we caught about as many smallmouth bass as you can catch in a day," he recalls. "It was as spectacular a day of fishing as I can remember. Most of the fish were below three pounds, but one fish, the one that got way, was certainly larger."

As Chris and friend Randy waded, they felt fish bump their legs.

"In retrospect, I'm sure they were redhorse suckers," he says. "At the time, however, we instantly thought they were smallies ready to chomp."

Randy dropped a jig-and-pig just as another fish brushed his leg, and instantly he locked into a fierce struggle.

"Randy probably had about four feet of line out, and he fought the fish as best he could," Gulstad explains. "He lifted her out of the water, and, lo and behold, she was the biggest smallmouth I've ever laid eyes on.

"The bronze behemoth was dangling by Randy's jig out of the water as we looked at each other in astonishment and sheer excitement. How big is it? Is it a state record? Can you believe it hit like that?"

Splash.

"She wiggled just enough to pull loose from Randy's jig," Gulstad says. "We never saw that fish again, but we'll always remember her."

Arkansas pro Kevin Short, meanwhile, has caught many larger bass than the one he lost awhile back at Lake Eufaula. He remembers it for another reason.

"It sticks in my mind the clearest because of where I was in the standings and how I felt it could have helped me move up," he remembers. "We get to the deepest stretch of grass in the creek, and I switch to a jig," Short says. "First flip, a bass picks it up and starts heading to deep water. I set the hook and know it's a good one. She rolls up to the top, and I see a fish in the 5- to 6-pound class."

The bass dives, then turns and shoots straight up. Following a jump, she speeds straight at the boat.

"As she's coming at the boat, for some reason I still can't fathom, I try to pull her in the same direction she's going," says the Arkansas angler. "Not one of my brighter moments. "Naturally, I pulled the jig straight out of her mouth. The bad part was, I knew when the jig came flying out what I'd done wrong. I should have kept pressure in the opposite direction. "I sat down in my boat in utter disgust."

My amateur partner said, "I was not impressed with that."

"No kidding."

Bill Dance knows well the feeling. As memorable to him as the Pickwick smallmouth is the bass he lost at Clarks Hill in 1973. He believes that fish would have won the Bassmaster Classic for him. Instead, he finished second to Rayo Breckenridge.

Time, though, has tempered the pain of losing both those fish, and helped Dance learn an important lesson about the value of fishing.

"It's not the pounds or numbers of fish you catch," he says. "Yes, you can weigh those, but they don't come close to the memories."

Among those memories are visions of the big ones caught—and others that got away—both of which help explain why we fish.

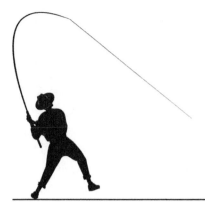

Chasing Rainbows

We got up at 4:15 a.m. to be on the water at five. Unfortunately, the fish didn't seem to care. Then the rain started. It wasn't all over. Mostly it was to the west and a little bit overhead.

In the east, where the sun hadn't yet moved above the horizon, the sky was mostly clear. Then came the magic. With the sun beaming up from below the skyline, my friend Norm Klayman and I watched the formation of the most spectacular rainbow either of us had ever seen.

Normally, I don't bother taking photos of rainbows. Even with digital, I've learned cameras just can't do them justice, but with this one, I had to try, even though it was far too large for me to photograph in its entirety. The picture turned out better than I expected. Still, it doesn't compare to what we saw with our own eyes.

If someone had asked me to get up at 4:15 to go see a rainbow, I might have said, "No, thank you. I've seen plenty of them." Yet I'm always ready to get up at those hours to go fishing. If I hadn't gone fishing on this morning, I would have missed a sight I will treasure for the rest of my life.

Of course, that rainbow isn't the only example of how nature has provided collateral enrichment during my time on the water. I could tell you about hundreds more. Probably you could do the same. Here are a few more of my favorite nature-inspired memories.

Closing my eyes, I once again smell the salt air and see those thousands of spinner dolphins that surrounded our boat off the Osa Peninsula in Costa Rica. Many sped right along beside us for awhile, leaping, rolling, and twisting in the characteristic way that gives them their names. Watching their jubilant acrobatics made me smile then, and the memory still brings happiness.

While fishing for bass along a rocky bank at Bull Shoals Lake, I looked up just in time to see a weasel streak from its den, grab a rabbit by the neck. and drag it out of sight. So deadly and efficient was the hunter that the rabbit never made a sound. If I hadn't looked up at that exact moment, I never would have been treated to this predatory scene right out of a National Geographic special.

While fishing from the back of the boat one winter in Florida's Crystal River, I watched with open mouth as a young manatee swam right up to the outboard and raised its head. Slowly kneeling down, I touched its cold flesh just above the eyes, and, in response, it rolled over on its back, allowing me to stroke its belly.

While angling on a lake in South Africa, three young otters also paid me a visit at the back of the boat. I didn't try to pet them— they're predators with sharp teeth, after all—but was content to watch them watch me, as they chattered and chattered. Finally, their mother showed up, fussed a bit, and escorted them away.

Back in Costa Rica, a guide drove a fishing buddy and me up into the cloud forests to go trout fishing. Enroute, he told us how birders from all over the world come to this mountainous area to see the elusive quetzal, a spectacular bird with gaudy blue-green plumage and a red breast.

After paved road turned to dirt, we stopped to talk to a couple of hikers. They were from the Netherlands, they said, and they had come to see a quetzal. During a week of searching the surrounding forest, they had yet to find one.

We wished them luck and slowly headed down the road toward the trout stream. The hikers were barely out of sight behind us when a quetzal flew across the trail in front of us.

Finally, this one ranks right up there with the rainbow at the top of my favorites: Twelve-year-old Jesse and I were fishing for bass from a pedal boat one dark summer night in the little lake behind my house. We were having a great time as we caught fish and quietly laughed about the bad casts we occasionally made into overhanging trees.

And then we saw them.

Along the woody shoreline in front of us, fireflies suddenly blinked in the grass. As we watched, they lit up all around the edge of the lake, circling us with delicate green fire.

"Cool!" Jesse exclaimed. Despite my college education and years of experience as an English teacher and a writer, I couldn't have said it any better, and I didn't try.

Anglers are also conservationists. They believe in
protection and sustainable use of our waters and fisheries.

I'm Not an Environmentalist

I'm for a stronger Clean Water Act. I want to preserve old-growth forests. I think it's a disgrace our federal government hasn't acted more decisively to keep invasive species out of the Great Lakes. I believe we need stiffer regulations to protect our streams from strip mining, our groundwater from herbicides, and our estuaries from the runoff pollution of urban sprawl and farm fields.

But, alas, I'm also an angler, and some of the reasons I fish also relate to why I don't call myself an environmentalist. I suspect many other anglers feel the same way.

It's not that we don't care about the environment. Rather, it's because we do care in a way environmentalists don't understand.

We don't want to be called "environmentalists" because we associate that description with agenda-driven campaigns for preservation policies that often are not backed by scientific evidence.

For anglers, "conservationist" is the term of choice. Conservationists believe in both protection and sustainable use of our lands, waters, and other natural resources. They follow an ethical code of behavior and embrace a stewardship philosophy.

So we have two factions, conservationists and environmentalists, sharing many of the same values, but more often viewing each other as enemies rather than allies.

For example, environmentalists embrace a strategy to use Marine Protected Areas and other designations by governments at all levels to deny recreational anglers access to public waters. In doing so, they are shamefully insulting and dismissing a constituency that does more to protect those waters than any other.

The California League of Conservation Voters (CLCV) compared the Partnership for Sustainable Oceans (PSO) to the Tobacco Institute because the PSO is opposed to a rush-to-judgment approach on closing California coastal waters to recreational angling. The CLCV said PSO "is nothing more than a front group for the fishing industry and boat manufacturers that are more interested in short-term profits than the long-term health of California's fisheries and marine life. Its misinformation campaign about the science of Marine Protected Areas and the hefty campaign contributions from its backers to anti-environment candidates in California show this industry group's true colors."

First, the fishing industry groups that support PSO are not endorsing a product that has killed millions and cost this nation billions of dollars in health-care costs. Rather, they are supporting a family-oriented recreational pastime enjoyed by about 40 million licensed anglers annually. This is an entry-way activity that has introduced generations of children to the beauty and pleasures of the outdoors.

Yes, these industries do profit from recreational fishing, but here's what the environmental groups fail to see, or choose not to see: Since 1952, fishermen have contributed more than $5 billion for betterment of our aquatic resources through the excise taxes they pay on the fishing equipment produced by those industries. Through the federal Sport Fish Restoration Program (SFR), the U.S. Fish and Wildlife Service distributes that money to the states for fisheries research, management, and stocking, as well as access improvements and expansions. Thanks to SFR, state wildlife agencies have acquired 360,000 acres for public enjoyment and taught aquatic education classes to more than 12 million people.

Environmental groups also fail or choose not to acknowledge the difference between recreational angling and commercial fishing. This suggests their agendas are not nearly as noble as they pretend. If they were solely motivated to protect our aquatic resources, they would work with recreational anglers who could be valuable partners, instead of demonizing them.

Organizations of like-minded individuals also desire to grow memberships and increase contributions to ensure their survival. Creating a crisis where one doesn't exist and focusing on enemies, real or imagined, are great ways to do this. Thus, the PSO is compared to the Tobacco Institute.

Here's the aggravating philosophical rub: anglers acknowledge that our oceans, lakes, and rivers possess incalculable intrinsic value. They appreciate spiritual restoration from nature as much as they appreciate the experience of catching fish. In fact, many fishermen view themselves as closet environmentalists because of this enjoyment of nature beyond the material. They believe this nation's natural resources have benefited from the environmental movement.

But die-hard environmentalists with tunnel vision believe humans exist apart from nature, rather than being part of it, and we act immorally when we disrupt nature in any way—and that includes recreational angling.

Undoubtedly, some waters—at times—should be closed to commercial fishing. With scientific research to support such a move, possibly some waters should be closed to recreational angling, at least temporarily. That's what brought back the striped bass fishery on the East Coast.

Yes, commercial fishing has decimated some fish stocks and destroyed fish habitat, but recreational anglers are stewards and environmental watchdogs for the waters upon which they fish. Some of us do keep fish to eat, but the majority today practice catch-and-release, knowing good fishing in the future depends on sound conservation practices today.

Yet President Barack Obama's Interagency Ocean Policy Task Force made no distinction between the two in its report on how to better protect oceans and the Great Lakes. Rather, high-level members from departments such as Commerce, Interior, and Homeland Security referred to "overfishing" and "unsustainable fishing." This time, ignorance was no excuse. Advocates of recreational angling made certain of that before the report was written.

Based on the task force's recommendations, the administration then created a National Ocean Policy to manage our oceans, coastal waters, and the Great Lakes, with ambiguous wording that will permit federal intrusion inland as well. As with the task force, the council is populated with and/or heavily influenced by those who follow "environmental" dogma, as opposed to those who see and appreciate the multiple values provided by the nation's angler conservationists.

As a consequence, anglers could lose access to thousands of miles of public waters in the years to come, as those same waters lose their most stalwart champions.

That's why anglers aren't environmentalists.

I Am a Steward

I love to fish. I live to fish. And I want to ensure future generations have many opportunities to spend quality time on the water. That's why I'm a steward. Here's how I live my life:

- I recycle everything I possibly can recycle—newspaper, junk mail, plastic, glass, and cardboard. I accumulate one small bag (Walmart size) of trash about every month or so.

- I compost. Fruit and vegetable wastes go onto my land to enrich the soil.

- I don't use fertilizer or pesticides on my lawn. In fact, "lawn" might not be the proper word for my yard. A portion of it gets mowed every couple of weeks, but the rest remains natural.

- Along my lakeshore, I maintain a buffer zone to prevent erosion.

- When branches occasionally break off the big oak trees on my property, I place them on brush piles I have scattered around as refuges for birds and small animals.

- I conserve energy by turning off lights, closing doors, etc.

- I fix dripping faucets promptly, and I don't leave the water running as I brush my teeth.

- I drive a car that gets 36 miles per gallon.
- I pick up other people's trash.
- I report polluters.
- I am a member of Recycled Fish, a conservation organization devoted to living a life of stewardship because we all live downstream.

Fulfilling the Inner Fisherman
Dr. Bruce Condello

(Dr. Bruce Condello is a noted expert on aquaculture and private pond management. He is a frequent contributor to Pond Boss Magazine, *and owns* BigBluegill.com *website. He has been featured in* In-Fisherman Magazine.)

Surely, we as humans have few, if any, similarities to insects. Human have the ability to plan, love, worship, and dream. Termites eat wood. Humans create, strategize, and build rocket ships. Ants build little hills.

By nature's standards, however, termites and ants are every bit as successful as we humans are. When success is measured by durability and longevity, it's hard to argue that we are a superior species.

Upon first blush, humans and insects are wildly different, but deeper analysis offers some profound similarities. Both species are social beings. Both are highly adaptive. Just because we can dream and love doesn't mean we're any more likely to survive a nuclear holocaust. The insects are great at what they do.

We all know adolescent termites don't fight over the opportunity to be warriors, workers, or royalty. Their caste system is simply a matter of genetic birthright. Their social hierarchy has nothing whatsoever to do with choice. Each of their responsibilities is equally important to maintaining the integrity, efficiency, and viability of the collective whole. Each social function is co-dependent on all the other functions.

So why would it be hard to imagine that human societies function in largely the same way? It seems intuitive that some humans have a "birthright" to certain social tasks and functions.

Sociologists have long recognized the need in pre-industrial societies for humans to have the ability to fulfill the different, but equally important roles of hunter-gatherer, leader, warrior, facilitator, and laborer. Perhaps deep in our DNA lies a need for some people to capture, and even kill. Perhaps going to the local grocery store to buy a can of Spam doesn't quite give us dispensation from this deep-seeded need. Catch a fish, and maybe you get to place a little checkmark on your emotional "to-do" list.

Drilling into deep socio-psychological arguments like this is more likely to produce heat than light, but the question has already been asked ... Why do we fish?

And why is this such a difficult question to answer? It seems that 40 million folks in the United States—a veritable angling army— might have a single overriding motivation, but asking ten avid anglers why they fish is likely to evoke eleven different answers.

So is DNA hardwiring the twelfth answer? If it's true that some folks are born to fish, it would follow that certain people possess an equally mysterious motivation to perform other tribal-specific tasks.

Gardening might be a good place to start. If there's a cellular-level need to gather, it would stand to reason that some folks garden for no other good reason. There would be people who live near perfectly good grocery stores who feel a deep-seeded need to bury a dried pea in the ground.

Check.

And what about leading? If there is a DNA-level desire among some to lead and preside, there would be millionaires who spend their fortune to gain office.

Double check.

How about fighting and defending? If there's primordial need for some people to defend, certain people would be some who leave well-paying jobs, beautiful wives, and girlfriends to enter the battlefield.

Pat Tillman comes to mind.

Now if you're going to try to get your spouse to endorse an upcoming fishing trip by telling her you're just following your genes, then good luck. Take comfort in reminding yourself that Van Gogh's wife probably wanted him to take out the trash more often, and that Walt Whitman's wife was probably irritated that he refused to oil that squeaky back door.

By the same token, don't feel bad if you think you might have a crush on your fly rod. You may not be able to help it.

Unfortunately, if you're going to accept the argument that some in the human population are born fishermen, you'll have to also accept that others are born "not-fishermen." The segment of the population who would rob us of our right to fish and hunt may be selfish, constitutionally ignorant rubes, but no amount of reading, education, or experience will ever allow them to feel how we feel when it comes to the pursuit and capture of fish. It's quite likely their archetypal calling just doesn't include fishing. They may never forgive us for wanting to catch fish, but we'll just have to forgive them for not understanding how we feel.

The Campfire

Huddled around the campfire, the tribe gathers up. Meat needs a little extra time to digest, so it looks like there's going to be an extended story time. The last group around the fire—and the tightest group of friends—are the hunters and fishermen.

Why is that?

Because there's a need to review and sort out the successes of the day. There's also a need to create strategies that will assure successes tomorrow. Without this primordial water cooler, nothing is learned, nothing is passed on, and nothing is added to the cultural heritage of the group.

But there's one less obvious impetus for these meetings. Spouses and potential spouses are within hearing distance. The storyteller with the best capture rate and the best flair for describing the events has the ear of the more "fishing-challenged" opposite sex members. Successful hunters equate easily to being the best providers for baby fly fishermen. The "hunt for game" fluidly shifts back and forth to "hunt for spouse." By these means, the DNA for fishermen gets locked into each subsequent generation.

The Fishing Archetype

An archetype is an idea or thought embedded in the collective human consciousness. Some people call it instinct. Others feel the word "instinct" doesn't apply to humans. Regardless, you don't have to know anything about snakes or spiders to get creeped-out when you're around them. Nor do you need someone to tell you that a Mom is a good thing. As a child you see Mom, and you love Mom. Archetypes give children a head start during that scary and difficult 15 years of growing up. Archetypes help us decide what to fear, what to love, and what to do.

Deep in the human consciousness lies the hunting and fishing archetype. The Greek philosopher Plato believed ideas were pure forms imprinted on your soul before you were even born. Plato would have understood the fisherman. The fisherman doesn't necessarily know why he fishes. He'll try to articulate it, but when the words come out, they don't seem to quite do justice to how he feels. When he's speaking the words to another fisherman, a smile comes across the other angler's face, and he nods gently and sincerely. If those same words are spoken to a non-angler, there's always the same perplexed response. It's a look that says, "When they were handing out archetypes, I was in line for an ice cream cone somewhere."

If this fishing archetype isn't embedded in your soul before birth, you can become a successful angler, but never a true fisherman. If you try to teach your child to be an avid fisherman, perhaps passing on the correct DNA gives you a little better chance of a successful outcome, but ultimately, if the genes aren't there, don't blame yourself. It's not going to happen. Being a true fisherman may be a little like having blue eyes or brown hair.

Saying we fish because it's in our deepest chemical level doesn't sound very romantic. It's a little like saying we fish because we have to, but saying we fish because our DNA requires us to doesn't mean there can't be a multitude of other reasons as well. We eat because we're hungry, but that doesn't mean we don't also smell the wonderful aromas of Grandmother's cherry pie. We eat to survive, but we also appreciate the visual presentation created by a master chef.

Where Can We Take This?

The highest directive we could take from this theory is that each and every child in this country should have exposure to the sport of angling. There are surely millions of children who will never get a chance to satisfy their inner fisherman. Without the proper exposure, it would be easy to imagine these children growing up and feeling they've missed out on something—on the deepest emotional level. Maybe a few million more youth fishing trips would mean tens of millions fewer trips to the psychologist.

Think about it. If you were really, truly meant to be something and never had the chance, could you ever be fulfilled? If it was etched in your DNA that you should hunt, but you never smelled country air, what would that mean to you?

Having each and every current angler take two or three kids fishing every year would only be the smallest of burdens. If you've never seen the unfolding of a human psyche first exposed to hunting or fishing, you're missing one of the greatest joys and opportunities of your life. Make it happen!

A penguin's passion for bubbles reveals how much we still
don't know about other species.

Partying With Penguins

Back in the 1990s, I went to South Africa and other countries in the southern half of Africa. Primarily I went to see and photograph the wildlife, although I also made time for fishing.

Fishing led me into photography and photography led me to Africa, where I met the African penguin, also known as the black-footed penguin or, my favorite name, the jackass penguin. The latter is based on its donkey-like bray.

I met my favorite penguin again while I was in Sarasota, Florida, for a Theodore Roosevelt Conservation Partnership saltwater media summit. Mote Marine Laboratory was a co-sponsor, and the good folks there took us behind the scenes to see the stars of an exhibit, Penguin Island.

One of the penguins meandered about us, reminding me of a curious little child. Then a staffer pulled out a bottle of bubbles. The penguin was fascinated by them, moving its bill to within inches of a cluster and solemnly watching as they drifted away.

Someone said that possibly penguins are drawn to bubbles because they remind them of bubbly sea foam. Maybe that's the case.

But what this tells me is that learning to relate to other species is a riddle wrapped inside an enigma, and we have just begun. I'm not saying that someday we will have meaningful conversations with penguins, pollock, and porcupines. I am saying that life is a mystery that we are only beginning to unravel and sometimes we're treated to a glimpse at what's behind the curtain.

When I told him the penguin story, Leonard Sonnenschein, a good friend who's also an internationally recognized fisheries expert, put it another way: "We don't think of animals as having self-awareness when we see them in groups, but when we see one by itself, we realize some of them do."

That reminded me of the behavior of a bowfin I used to watch when I did volunteer work at the St. Louis World Aquarium. A bowfin, also called mudfish and many other names, is a primitive predator that dates all the way back to the Jurassic period.

One day, I realized it was watching me right back from its home in a low, wide tank. It wasn't just that it followed me as I walked along the edge of the enclosure. Such behavior easily can be attributed to conditioning for food. With this fish, it seemed more than that. When I stood at the edge of the tank and looked down at the bowfin, it looked up at me with eyes that seem to be pondering a riddle.

Anthropomorphization? Maybe. Attributing human character-istics is an easy thing to do, especially with species we spend considerable time around. Look at how many in our society treat dogs and cats, and I spend a lot of time around fish.

Besides fishing, I used to keep home aquariums, and one of my favorite fish was the Oscar, a South American cichlid. It too exhibited an awareness of what was going on outside its watery realm. In fact, aquarium books cite examples of these fish being taught to ring bells and perform tricks in exchange for food.

I never tried that. But I did see something just as impressive at a marina. I don't remember which lake, but if this happens at one of them, likely it happens at several. The owner trained a bass to jump through a hoop in exchange for minnows. He could confirm that it always was the same fish by a black spot on its tail.

Is all of this an argument against fishing and supporting animal rights? No, it is not. I'm simply pointing out that, as the dominant species on this watery planet, we don't know nearly as much as we think we do.

Actually, this is an argument to spend more time angling, not just because it's fun but because, in doing so, we learn more about nature and, as a consequence, become even better stewards.

Also, fishing keeps us humble, which makes us better people. Infrequent success reminds us we have much to learn from creatures less "intelligent" than ourselves.

Big bass like this 12-pounder don't break lines. Anglers do.

Own Your Mistakes

O ver the years, I've heard dozens of anglers say big fish broke their lines.

That's it, end of discussion. "Nothing that I could have done," they say. "I'll have better luck next time."

If that's what you want to believe, go ahead. If you buy into the "bad luck" mentality, it will happen to you again. And again. And again.

Heck, losing a big one is going to occur from time to time no matter what you do and no matter how good you are, if you fish often enough. Howeve, you will lose fewer fish when you take responsibility for what happens when you hook one.

Ready for an attitude adjustment? Then remember this: fish do NOT break the line. You do. Maybe you set your drag too tight or pulled too hard on the rod. Maybe you didn't retie when you should have, or put on new line as often as you should.

How do I know this? I'm the voice of experience.

While fishing in the Amazon I watched in stunned amazement as a huge peacock blasted my Woodchopper right by the boat, charged away, and popped my 80-pound braid as if it were kite twine. Instead of line peeling off my reel after the fish hit, it buried into the spool and snapped. From that I learned not to crank down the drag as tight on braid as on monofilament or copolymer line.

On Lake Comedero in Mexico, a double-digit largemouth clobbered my Chug Bug about 30 feet out. I didn't lose this one; the guide did. While the fish was still green, he took a swipe at it with the net and knocked it free.

That's when I made my mistake. I didn't retie. On the next cast, what appeared to be an equally large bass grabbed my topwater bait—and the line snapped.

I've also seen some stunning mistakes by others. My favorite is the guy who is more concerned with boating his catch than enjoying the fight. In one quick motion, he tries to hoist and swing a large fish aboard as it comes toward the boat, but the fish weighs too much for such a maneuver and the rod breaks, typically with a "pop" that sounds like a gunshot.

I've seen this happen four times. I never tire of being amused by such self-destructive impatience.

Last summer, my friend across the lake didn't make that mistake, but he did lose a big catfish, as did I, while fishing off his dock. He lost the first one. It was about ten feet from the dock, too far for us to see how big it actually was. Suddenly the line snapped.

"Man, that had to be a big one," he said. "This is braided line."

That was the end of the story for him, but here's what I saw: he was using a rod and reel with line that had been baking in the sun all summer on his dock. He wasn't using the rod to fight the fish. It was pointed almost straight at the fish when the line parted.

A few days later, I lost one from the same dock. The difference was that mine headed straight for brush we've placed along the edge of a dropoff. The drag was as tight as I dared turn it, and, just as the fish neared the brush, my rod stopped it.

For a few seconds, we were at stalemate. If I had just been patient, I probably could have turned that fish and caught it.

Instead, I pulled back on the rod just a bit, and the line snapped. The fish didn't break that line; I did.

Ask my friend what happened to us last summer, and he will tell you that big fish broke our lines.

Ask me, and I'll tell you we both made mistakes that cost us fish.

Now you tell me who's more likely to catch one of those big catfish from his dock this summer.

One of the reasons that we fish is because it is fun.

Lessons Learned from Fishing
By Kathy Magers

(One of the most respected women anglers, Kathy Magers was a 2005 inductee into the Legends of the Outdoors Hall of Fame and a 2002 inductee into the Texas Freshwater Fishing Hall of Fame. She was a Bass'n Gal National Champion and once guided former President George W. Bush on a six-hour fishing trip.)

Why Do We Fish?

That's a question I've asked myself repeatedly over the years, especially when fishing in cold, rainy weather, with ice clogging the eyelets on my rod. Or baking in the sun, or having driven thousands of miles to compete in a tournament in which I did poorly. But for me, fishing is what kryptonite was to Superman.

My first fishing trip was at age four; the most recent came after I deposited my Social Security check in the bank before leaving town. What happened in between represents six decades of fishing, and each was a life lesson for adulthood.

The first decade taught me patience; the second, self-confidence; the third, to share with family and friends; the fourth, to challenge myself on a professional level; and the fifth, to give back to the sport. Now, in my sixth angling decade, I'm learning to relax and fish for fun once again, dampening the fast-paced competitive tendency of my past. I competed on all the women's national tours such as Bass'n Gal, Lady Bass, Women's Bass Fishing Association and Women's Bassmaster Tour. Fishing is a fantastic teaching tool and bonding agent.

We Fish for Fun

In my case, it was the lure of the cork going under.

"When it goes under, pull!" Grandpa would say. I'd watch intently for movement with never a blink of the eye, holding every breath until I must have turned blue. Then finally, a nibble created water rings around the cork and sent my heart fluttering like a scared hummingbird. Then, poof! My cork was under!

If you fish, you know the rest of the routine: Shouts of "reel fast!" and "set the hook!" I missed many fish early on because it was hard to reel and giggle at the same time. As I aged, my catch rate improved. I never realized how our family bonded on those trips or that I was learning patience—a positive attribute in life and worm fishing.

I don't think children's fishing rods and reels existed when I was little. Maybe that's why Grandpa handed me a full-size saltwater rod equipped with an open-faced reel at age six. Yes, six. Some adults struggle to master open-faced reels. Mean old Grandpa (so I thought) told me to put my thumb on the reel line when my bait neared the water so it wouldn't backlash. I didn't listen. He was nice enough to untangle the first dozen backlashes, but eventually I heard "The next time you don't listen to me, you're on your own."

Guess I called his bluff, and there I was red-faced and sobbing "I can't do this!" Eventually, when no one babied me, the tangles came out and I was praised for doing it myself. I learned that day to listen or pay the consequences in life. I also learned that no matter how messed up something in life seems, it eventually straightens out—if you just keep working on it.

Beauty to Behold

While most of my little friends were fast asleep at 4 a.m. on a Saturday, I felt special when mom whispered "Wake up, sleepy head. We're going fishing with Grandpa in the boat."

I sprang from bed and into my clothes like a cheetah. Breakfast followed at a beachfront café, where, to this day, I remember the chin-high Formica table top, the scooting sounds of metal chairs, and the smell of fresh brewed coffee in the air.

We then rode a ferry from Galveston Island over to Port Bolivar. Dad would lift me up to look over the side at neon-glowing phosphorous breaking atop the ferry wake. Porpoises raced alongside us—a huge thrill for me. So there I was, with the salty gulf breeze blowing my pig tails, experiencing the most breathtaking nature scenes framed by swirling seagulls and pelicans everywhere. I saw shrimp boats in the distance, a cloudy peach sky swirled with gray clouds, punctuated with a hot, red ball of sun—all while my friends slept. I doubt the adults realized what deep impressions those trips etched in my young mind. Even today, I'm sure I'm not alone when I say nature and its beauty is a major reason I fish.

Boating Goes With Fishing

When I was good, Grandpa let me steer the boat back across the bay. I could barely see anything, so I stretched my neck giraffe style to see over the salty, frosted windshield. I vividly recall him teaching me to "quarter" the waves at an angle instead of hitting them head on, getting us wet. That lesson absolutely saved my life in rough waters year later when a Kentucky weather front blew in three hours early and caught tournament boaters off-guard.

What a shame Grandpa died before I became a touring pro. More than once as I planed out and headed up a river or across a lake, I felt the wind in my ears and remembered the times I drove Grandpa's boat. Those were special times that nurtured my love of boating. In later years, I even became a registered Texas Boating Safety

Instructor and created my own annual women's boating courses in Dallas. As a touring pro I boated for decades, representing boat and motor manufacturers and dealers at boat shows. All because I steered Grandpa's boat for a few minutes at age six.

We Fish to Catch Fish

As a child, it was frightening, but fun, to catch a "monster fish" with both eyes on one side of its head (a saltwater flounder.) Or the "croaker" that barked like a dog. (Dad said he must have been chasing a catfish.) I caught a redfish that wasn't red at all, but gray, and a snapper that was red.

I got hooked in Las Vegas at age eight. I was an Air Force brat who landed a five-pound bass at Lake Mead. It was the largest fish caught out of four adults and me. Memories of that day flooded my mind as I looked out the airplane window over Lake Mead on my way to an industry trade show in Vegas.

In 1979, I discovered Bass'n Gal, the original women's professional fishing tour and joined the group, with my husband Chuck's full support. Thus, we began another decade in which fishing played an important role in our lives. Pro fishing gave us an opportunity to spend quality time traveling to six events per year. I enjoyed the challenge of our yellow-brick-road that stretched from Texas to New York, Florida, and nearly every state in between.

Fishing opened a door for me and my family that allowed me to meet governors, guide George Bush (our 43rd president), and film with legendary baseball pitcher Nolan Ryan. My pro career was the most rewarding result of taking the road less traveled in our sport.

We Fish for One-on-One Time

I spend a lot of time going to movies with my husband, shopping with our daughters, and watching our grandchildren play sports, but never feel closer to them than when we share a day on the lake. Chuck and I used to drop the girls off at school on Monday, our only day off, then spend our day fishing. On the water we shared uninterrupted time, a rare occasion in those days. I loved the slow pace and eating a picnic lunch on the water. We miss those days and look forward to more of them in retirement.

Mom occasionally accompanied me as my official practice partner on tour. No barking dogs, meals to cook, ringing phones, or doorbells to interrupt us. We would talk about life, and she shared tips on everything from motherhood to being a good wife. We still laugh about the day a beautiful powder blue dragonfly landed on the edge of my rod box as I dug, head down through it, looking for a different reel.

Mom said, "Oh, Kathy, look at that beautiful dragonfly."

I picked up the reel and asked, "Where?" as I slammed the rod box lid. We both gasped, but when I opened the lid, away it flew, unharmed. That day, I learned about luck.

With our grandsons, I learned something else. At ages seven and eight, they couldn't carry on a phone conversation. Every question from me was answered with "uh-huh," "I don't know," or "kinda." Only when I asked if they wanted to go fishing did the pace change, and, once in the boat, conversation never ceased.

"Gramma, do fish drink water?"

"Why is water wet?"

"Can I cast your fishing rod?"

These conversationally-challenged kids were all mine for the day. I especially loved times when they asked, "Can I steer the boat, Grandma?" Memories of Grandpa and Galveston Bay flooded back, and, when I said "Last cast!" my heart jack-hammered when they begged and pleaded for, "Just one more cast, Grandma! P-l-e-a-s-e?"

Fishing and boating were definitely the glue that bonded our family. One-on-one time with someone you care about is priceless.

We Fish to Grow the Sport

Bass'n Gal was founded around the time of the women's liberation movement. Consequently, as we attempted to grow women's role in fishing, we were labeled as bra-burning libbers, which we were not. We wanted support from the industry, yet some believed we were rocking the boat by trying to force our way into a man's sport. Those days weren't always easy, being out there on the water was *so* much more fun than waving our husbands off to fish, and then sitting idly on the bank until they returned.

Of course, the men, mine included, always asked as we women came to weigh in if we'd hit anything on the lake with our boats. Even when I said no, Chuck was crawling up under the hull to make sure. As time passed, our guys became not only confident in our fishing and boating skills, but dared anyone to make a negative comment about us, and they boasted about our abilities to back up our boats.

In the following years, we realized that unlike our male counterparts, we needed better fitting clothing and equipment. Boys sizes didn't do the job since they were straight as a board and we were curvy. Year after year, we were ignored and seldom taken seriously.

We realized that creating demand was the best way to help manufacturers see us as a target market. We didn't want pink clothes—just functional outerwear for cold weather. We wanted respect on the water, to be looked at as capable boaters and anglers rather than "eye candy" sunning on the back boat deck. We noticed in fishing and boating ads that women were always passengers, never drivers. Ads showed only boys fishing with dads or grandpas.

Where were the girls and how would our daughters ever grow up to know the sport was theirs, too? Super sponsors like Mercury Marine, Ranger Boats, Motor Guide, Zebco-Quantum, and others led the way in supporting us. Eventually, women showed up in national ads as boaters and anglers. Clothing companies began to hear us.

I remember 10-X brand came out with women's rain suits. We loved them! They had rooms for our curves and our pants legs no longer dragged the ground. Our presence in those days decades back most definitely contributed to the positive changes we see in fishing today. Young women who like to fish are no longer embarrassed to admit it. Society's perspective of women who fish changed drastically and, today, we are recognized consumers and anglers.

For all of these reasons and more, fishing is a timeless passion I love with all my heart.

This toothy barracuda took a bait intended for tarpon.

You Just Never Know

*H*eat and drought have pushed the bass and most of the bluegill out to deeper water in the little lake behind my house. Also, too many years of catching big bass on topwaters, spinnerbaits, and swimbaits at Lake El Salto in Mexico have spoiled me; mining the depths with finesse baits just isn't appealing.

So I've been heading over to my neighbor's dock once or twice a week to fish with him for bluegill, catfish, and—my favorite!–grass carp. He has an automated feeder that throws out pellets at 6:30 and again at 9:00. The fish start gathering there about 6, along with turtles, ducks, and even a muskrat for the second feeding.

Only problem is, the fish have become so conditioned to eating pellets that they now ignore worms and even the bread balls I offer the carp. My friend turned off the feeder for a week and we tried fishing again last night, hoping they'd be more cooperative. A few bluegills ate worms, as did a big softshell turtle, but both catfish and carp still wouldn't touch our baits.

Finally, about 8:30, a few dimples started to appear on the surface of the calm, clear lake. Hoping I could entice a big bluegill or a small bass, I started throwing a small minnow bait with an ultralight. That wasn't my first choice, but it was rigged and ready.

About the fourth or fifth cast, with the bait only a few feet from the dock, a long, gray fish suddenly dashed out of deeper water and grabbed it.

The fish turned out to be a 5-pound-plus channel catfish, not bad for 6-pound line and a buggy whip rod.

That surprise element is one of the most appealing things about fishing for me; it can come at any moment.

While fishing for bass in Oklahoma a few years ago, I caught a 20-pound-plus flathead catfish on a spinnerbait. Aside from the enormity of the fish, what I remember most is that I mistakenly handled it as I would a bass. I held it up vertically for photos and then, with both hands in its mouth, started to lower it gently into the water for release. Suddenly, it thrashed violently, escaped my grasp, and crashed into the water, not only drenching me, but leaving the fingers on both of my hands raw and bleeding.

Up in Nebraska, I caught a 20-4 northern pike on a plastic crawfish in the shallow backwaters of the Missouri River during a hot August day. Most anglers and fisheries biologists would tell you the odds of such a fish being in such a place during the summer heat were infinitesimal, but it was there. I'll always remember how it exploded from the cattails and then greyhounded across the water.

In the Florida Keys, I dueled a goliath grouper for 45 minutes, after it ate a small fish I was reeling in. At least the captain and crew on the headboat think it was a goliath. We never saw the fish. I'm not sure it ever knew it was hooked, although I pulled and pulled with my drag cranked down as tight as I dared on the 30-pound line. Finally, knowing the risk, I put a deeper bend into the rod—and it cracked like a rifle shot. A broken rod, an empty reel, a sore elbow—and a fight I'll never forget—were my souvenirs from that adventure.

Below a dam in Illinois, I fought a mammoth bighead carp for even longer after it inhaled my crappie jig. It was almost within my grasp when the 6-pound line finally parted and a collective "Ahhhhh!" spontaneously erupted from the crowd that surrounded me.

In Costa Rica, however, the big one didn't get away. Call it beginner's luck. On my first trip to the Central America country, I walked a beach on the Caribbean side, throwing a black/pink jig—a local favorite—for snook. I was using a 6-foot medium action rod and 14-pound line on a small capacity reel, gear far better suited for bass than snook.

Sadly, the snook weren't biting, but a tarpon was. It ate my jig, nearly yanked the rod out of my hand, and then rocketed toward deep water. All I could do was hold on. I knew I couldn't stop the fish, no matter how skillfully I played it. I waded out into the water as far as I dared, knowing as I did so that it was a pointless gesture.

But then the miraculous occurred, just as I looked down at my reel to see all the line gone except for the knot. The tarpon hit the wall of waves crashing about 80 yards out at the breakline. The waves and the admittedly puny pressure from my undersize rod were just enough to turn the fish and I started gaining line. I managed to work the tarpon to within a few feet of me before it leaped and headed out to sea once more.

I don't know how many times this happened, but it was more than twice, and each time that fish turned just as I saw the knot. If the wall of waves had been another foot farther out or I hadn't waded out as far as I did, the tarpon easily would have broken off. But it didn't.

Eventually it tired enough for me to bring within reach, and I actually touched the fish, making it an official catch. Watching from the beach, the guide estimated its weight at 85 pounds. Just as he did so, the tarpon made one last dash and the line parted.

Finally, way back during my college years, I was bringing in a small bass that had eaten my topwater. As I reeled it the last couple of feet to shore, a tremendous explosion showered me with water and a fierce yank nearly pulled the rod from my hands. I never saw what ate the little bass and nearly hooked itself on my lure, but that brief moment in time will be forever with me.

When you throw out that bait ... you just never know.

Trash violates the natural beauty of scenes like this.

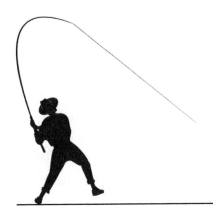

Trash Talk

*A*s with many of us who fish, I used to complain when I'd see trash along a shoreline or riverbank. The more I complained, the angrier I'd get about the people who give pigs a bad name.

One of the reasons we go to the lake, river, or ocean is to escape the pace, the noise, and the clutter of civilization. Seeing garbage tarnishing these pastoral places steals that peace of mind we seek in angling and reminds us too much of the negative aspects of our species.

If that's not enough, trash thrown on the ground eventually ends up in our waters, and, from my research as a conservation writer, I know that means hundreds of tons of garbage. For example, Keep America Beautiful says 51 billion pieces of litter are discarded on our roadways each year.

Finally, though, I realized that no matter how many articles I write, pleading with people not to trash our roads, our lands, and waters, it won't make any difference. Those who do such things don't read, don't care, or are unconscious in their daily lives.

But investigation revealed some good news: In my own state of Missouri, Stream Team volunteers removed 573 tons of trash from rivers and streams during 2011. Missouri River Relief, another volunteer campaign, picked up 676 tons from 800 miles of the Missouri River in six states, from 2001 to 2011.

I've never been a joiner, but those good people inspired me. I started picking up the garbage myself, and that has made all the difference in my personal happiness and at least a little in protecting our fisheries.

This past summer, I kicked it up a notch. I decided to walk to beaches at two nearby fishing lakes every morning and pick up the trash—as well as a few goodies that also get left behind. In addition to plenty of Styrofoam cups, food wrappers, plastic bottles, aluminum cans, and one disposable diaper, I've found the following in less than two weeks:

Beach toys—two swim masks, three pairs of goggles, two float tubes, and a toy-size personal watercraft.

Fishing tackle and outdoor accessories—a Cypress Gardens life jacket, a folding chair, a chartreuse buzzbait, two bobbers, and too much discarded monofilament line.

Reading material—a copy of a book by Ann Coulter entitled *If Democrats Had Any Brains, They'd Be Republicans*. (I am not making this up.)

Clothing—two pair of swim trunks, two pair of flip flops, a pair of plaid sneakers with ribbons for shoe laces, a flowered shirt and, oh yes, a large, black bra. (I am not making this up either; I don't even want to know how it came to be there.)

I now have quite an assortment of items to add to my next garage sale, and the lakes where I often fish are cleaner. Also, I have regained the peace of mind I allowed the slobs to steal from me. I'm not saying picking up what others leave behind is as much fun as fishing. Far from it, but taking control, being a caretaker for my fisheries, has healed my heart and lowered my blood pressure.

If seeing trash at your favorite fishing hole angers you, try picking it up. You'll feel better for it, I promise. Together we can make a difference—one large, black bra at a time.

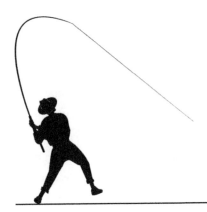

No Fishing?

Why do we fish? We can fill books with the reasons. An increasing number of people don't know about those reasons or even care about the incalculable value we derive from angling, both individually and as a society. Additionally, many are working diligently to keep us from enjoying this family-oriented pastime. For example, recreational fishing as we know it no longer exists in portions of Western Europe. Even more disturbing, the seeds of its destruction are well established here.

"Whether by design and intent or by other less nefarious means, I believe the very basis of science-based fish and wildlife management, conservation, and sustainable use is being threatened as never before," says Phil Morlock, Shimano's Director of Environmental Affairs.

"Many of the most effective antis are never strident about it, which is why they are such a threat," Morlock continues. "The agenda is to never appear to have an agenda."

Don't be misled by the fact that nine out of ten Americans approve of legal fishing and support using fish for food. When people are asked whether they approve of recreational fishing for sport, the answers dramatically change. Twenty-five to 30 percent view angling for sport as cruel in more urbanized states such as Colorado and

Arizona, while about 20 percent feel the same way in more rural states, including Alaska and the Dakotas.

Those disturbing revelations come from researchers in Germany, Switzerland, and the United States, who recently compiled their findings in a report entitled, "A Primer on Anti-Angling Philosophy and Its Relevance for Recreational Fisheries in Urbanized Societies."

Such attitudes, the authors say, raise the possibility "that extremist positions (or elements thereof) influenced by animal liberation or animal rights arguments might find their way into nongovernmental organizations, science, politics, and ultimately legislation.

"Such a development is particularly challenging for recreational fishers when it occurs where they have little political support. Without sufficient support, radical claims portraying anglers as cruel sadists who play with fish for no good reason can be rhetorically effective."

Why is this happening?

Basically, the answer is that attitudes change regarding fish and wildlife as people move away from nature and into more urban settings. Their beliefs become guided more by what they see on television and in the movies than what they personally experience.

Anglers and hunters view fish and wildlife as resources to be used, while being managed wisely and treated with respect. Traditionally, most Americans have agreed with that "utilitarian" philosophy.

As people become more urbanized (and often more affluent), some begin to favor a "mutualism wildlife value orientation, viewing wildlife as capable of relationships of trust with humans, as if part of an extended family, and as deserving of rights and caring."

Mutualists, the authors say, "are more likely to view fish and wildlife in human terms, with human personalities and characteristics."

What's coming down the road in the United States if mutualism prevails?

The Swiss Animal Welfare Act of 2008 highlights the nightmarish possibilities. The legislation makes catch-and-release illegal because "it is in conflict with the dignity of the fish and its presumed ability to suffer and feel pain."

A similar rule has been in place since the 1980s in Germany, where anglers also must take a course in fish handling before they can obtain a license.

"The argument runs that it is legally acceptable to go fishing only if one has the intention to catch fish for food," the study says.

"Wider economic benefits created by angling are usually not considered a sufficient justification—it all boils down to the individual benefits experienced by the angler, and here food provision is currently the only acceptable reason."

In other words, recreational fishing as millions of Americans now enjoy it is not allowed.

What would imposition of such a system in the United States mean?

- It would mean that a majority of the nation's 60 million anglers would stop fishing.
- It would mean an end to family outings and buddy tournaments, and depressurizing at a local lake or pond for a few hours after work.
- It would mean the collapse of economies for coastal communities and cities along the Great Lakes, as well as hundreds of towns near popular inland lakes and reservoirs.

In the United States, more people fish than play golf and tennis combined, and, in doing so they support more than one million jobs.

Through license fees and excise taxes, recreational anglers contribute $1.2 billion annually "to preserve, protect, and enhance not just their sport, but also the environment that makes such sportfishing possible," the American Sportfishing Association says. "Across much of the country, angler dollars are the primary source for improving fish habitat, public access, and environmental education."

All that could be gone if we allow a minority who believe fishing is cruel to dominate the conversation and dictate policy.

"Powerful intervention is needed to counterbalance such tendencies in a society where hunting and fishing are becoming less prominent and where an increasing percentage of the public has lost contact with wildlife and nature," say the authors of the study.

What do we do about? We go fishing, of course, and, at every opportunity, we introduce someone new to the sport. We practice good stewardship through individual actions, as well as club activities—and we publicize accomplishments. Also, we make certain that decision makers at every level of government know about both the calculable and incalculable value of recreational fishing to individuals, families, and society.

The following categorizes the threats to fishing so that they can be more easily recognized—and opposed.

Animal Rights

First, animal rights groups do pose a greater threat than many realize. Represented by organizations such as People for the Ethical Treatment of Animals (PETA) and the International Fund for Animal Welfare, they oppose not only sport fishing, but use of animals in agriculture and medical research.

"More organizations drift closer to that (agenda) every year," says Gordon Robertson, Vice President of the American Sportfishing Association. "They follow the demographics, and just look at today's society; it's becoming more and more urbanized and detached from nature."

A message like "save the whales," he adds, resonates much more with a population "used to emergency messages" than does a plan for fisheries management.

Along with proclaiming their concern for whales, seals, and other sympathetic animals, however, these groups also assert that fish "are tortured just for sport," and they claim that "others (fish) are unintended victims who are maimed or killed simply because they were in the wrong place at the wrong time."

The use of "victims" and "who" in referring to fish is no accident.

The threat is heightened because many in the media tend to be sympathetic to these causes, Morlock says. Consequently, reporters often fail to interview credible scientists who can separate fact from fiction on issues such as whether fish feel pain when they are hooked.

"If fish did, they would be unable to eat many of the spiny/prickly creatures like crawfish and other fish (because of dorsal spines) that they survive on," Morlock explains. "That's a rather obvious point to those of us who fish or have a background in science. For those who do not, the media does a poor job of filling in the rather glaring gaps in information often inherent in animal rights campaigns."

Consequently, their arguments often are taken at face value when these groups insist not only that fish can feel pain, but can suffer from "fear and anticipation of physical pain."

None of that is true, according to most credible scientists.

"When a fish is hooked by an angler, it typically responds with rapid swimming behavior that appears to be a flight response," says Dr. James Rose, who has spent more than 30 years studying neurological responses to pain in animals. "Human observers sometimes interpret this flight response to be a reaction to pain, as if the fish was capable of the same kind of pain experience as a human."

But fish "don't have the brain systems necessary to experience pain," he says, adding that "flight responses of fish are a general reaction to many types of potentially threatening stimuli and can't be taken to represent a response to pain."

Preservation

Government agencies and environmental groups, meanwhile, present larger and more dangerous challenges.

For example, the National Park Service (NPS) has limited angler access at Cape Hatteras National Seashore and seems intent on doing much the same at Florida's Biscayne Bay. For its actions, it cites the need to protect species and habitat.

"The National Park Service likes people who drive through on paved roads, get out to look, and then drive on," says ASA's Robertson. "It doesn't like people who require a higher degree of attention, like anglers and snowmobilers."

Max Sandlin, a former representative from Texas and member of the Congressional Sportsman's Caucus, adds, "The National Park Service and some others seem solely and exclusively focused on preserving. They have little experience with hunting and fishing and they don't understand that people in those sports support conservation. They don't implement a broad enough mission. It's not just about preserving a pristine area; it's about enjoying and interacting with nature."

Preservation also is what drives many environmental groups and charitable foundations, including those that worked with the Obama administration to develop a National Ocean Policy, designed to zone uses of our waters. First and foremost on their agendas are implementation of marine protected areas and preserves, where recreational fishing and other sustainable uses are not allowed.

Their ranks include Oceana, World Wildlife Fund, Environmental Defense Fund, and Natural Resources Defense Council, as well as PEW Oceans Conservancy, Packard Foundation, Hewlett Foundation, and Gordon and Betty Moore Foundation.

Their actions don't suggest any appreciation for the value of recreational angling to society, economies, and conservation, but are they anti-fishing per se?

Shimano's Morlock thinks at least some in their ranks might be.

"After years of various fishing organizations pointing out these negative impacts (caused by closures) to key members of the environmental community, one could ask how it is that they continue to fail to consider the negative impacts of their efforts on recreational fishing," he says. "It would be reasonable to draw the conclusion at some point that these actions and initiatives by Big Green groups translate from incidental to intentional."

Considering that preservationists believe we should live apart from nature — to protect it — instead of living as part of nature, that's a logical assumption. Like animal rights groups, preservationists embrace an ideology based more on emotion than facts, and they're finding an increasingly receptive audience in today's urbanized society.

In fact, it's entirely reasonable to suspect that preservation is driving most of the threats, from attempts to ban lead fishing tackle to NPS actions and the National Ocean Policy.

"With urbanization, you see a detachment from the outdoors," says ASA's Robertson. "That lends to a lesser understanding of recreational fishing and management. Fishing still enjoys a high approval rating in survey after survey, but the drift from country to urban is a challenge."

More Dangers

Other threats are less direct, but no less real, with recreational fishing at risk of being collateral damage. The persistent campaign by some environmental groups to ban lead fishing tackle is one of the most troubling, as is the growing movement by government, environmental groups, and lake associations to restrict public access.

With the former, the Center for Biological Diversity and others insist that lead fishing tackle must be banned to protect loons and other waterfowl. Even though no scientific research supports the notion that bird populations are being harmed by lead weights and other items, they continue to file lawsuits and push for bans at the state and federal levels, as well as try to sway public opinion.

"Getting the lead out seems a quick and easy fix, but the evidence is not there," says Sandlin. "Anglers and hunters are good conservationists. Those who want to ban lead might be well intentioned, but their arguments are not well thought out. A debate needs to be based on sound science. We need to be vigilant about these kinds of issues because they can go to the very heart of fishing and hunting."

Much the same could be said about attempts to limit public access to public waters: the evidence is not there to justify the action. In pushing for locked gates at launch ramps, lake associations cite concerns about boaters introducing invasive species such a zebra mussels and Eurasian watermilfoil.

"But in doing that, they're creating a barrier between themselves and groups like B.A.S.S. that are working on solving the problem," says Tom Sadler, Managing Director of The Middle River Group, LLC and former Conservation Director for the Izaak Walton League of America. "In closing access, they hurt the community, and they hurt their neighbors. Anglers must be ready with persuasive facts."

Combat Tactics

No matter how popular recreational fishing remains in surveys, it cannot survive without aggressive support from individual anglers, fishing groups, and elected officials—educated elected officials.

"Too often we see a knee-jerk reaction (among government officials) to any sort of information presented about a declining population or some other perceived environmental problem," Sandlin says. "Many attempts to address these issues are well intentioned, but often are reactionary and lack a basis in sound science. It is critical that issues such as economic benefit, access to public lands, recreational opportunities, and similar matters be considered vital elements of proposed solutions to perceived problems—problems which, after further inspection, often don't exist."

The education process begins with the individuals and groups, extolling the "collateral benefits" that recreational angling provides, according to Sadler. They include clean water and healthy fisheries, as well as economic benefits.

"We have to look for ways, to better get that message out to the American people," Sadler said, "especially people who see fishing as a recreation easily replaced. We have to do more to support and empower groups like Recycled Fish, the Izaak Walton League, Trout Unlimited, B.A.S.S., and the Federation of Fly Fishers. These struggle for support, energy, and resources. We have to do what we can to talk to people other than the choir. Social media creates that opportunity."

Chris Horton of the Congressional Sportsman's Foundation adds that anglers must pay attention to issues and communicate with both their state and federal representatives regarding those issues.

"Through the network of state sportsmen's caucuses, as well as the Congressional Sportsmen's Caucus, we have legislators who are willing to protect and advance our angling heritage," he says.

"With 60 million anglers in this country, we have the ability to significantly impact legislative and administrative decisions regarding recreational angling—but your elected officials must hear from you."

Some of the best worms for fishing hide under cow patties.

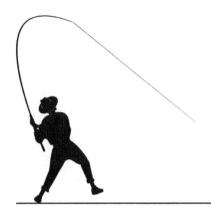

Worm Weather

Worm weather wasn't as good as Christmas, but, for a kid who loved to fish, it was a close second.

In early spring, drenching rains fell on thawing soil, forcing the wigglers to the surface to avoid drowning. Thus exposed, they were easy pickings on driveways and roads, and for at least a week or two, my friends and I had a bountiful supply of bait.

And what fun it was for us to chase after and pick up the slippery, slimy critters, and then try our best to keep them from squirming out of our hands as we conveyed them to the coffee can.

Decades later, I can't see a worm crawling across the road without reminiscing about worm weather and realizing that, when I was a kid, catching bait was a big part of the enjoyment of being a fisherman. I now know that, for a child, fishing opens the door to endless pleasure pursing worms, grasshoppers, crayfish, frogs, and minnows. In fact, much of the time, chasing live bait is probably more rewarding for youngsters than is the actual angling. Or to put it another way: catching bait helps affirm fishing as a positive experience for them.

At least that's how I remember it. We could almost always catch bait of some kind, while fooling fish was more problematic. I can recall stalking 'hoppers with a butterfly net and turning over rocks for crawdads as vividly—and with as much enjoyment—as I can recollect catching bluegills and bullheads with those baits.

One of my best memories is of the first day of summer vacation at the end of fifth grade. No sleeping in for me. I got up earlier than I would have for school, and three of us rode our bikes to a big tree in an open field at the edge of our subdivision. We had found lots of worms in the shade of that tree previously and were confident we'd find more that day. As I stood there with a shovel in my hand, I looked up at the early morning sun filtering through the branches and thought to myself that life just couldn't get much better than this.

I don't remember digging for the worms or anything else from that day. I just recall the simple moment in time when I was beginning an endless summer by digging worms with my friends so we could go fishing. That was perfection.

In truth, acquiring worms and using them for bait is a messy business, especially where fingernails are concerned. Of course, I didn't mind, but my mother did, especially at supper. I never told her about all of the worms we found by turning over cow patties in a nearby pasture. Or that sometimes the patties weren't quite as dry as they appeared to be. And, with hindsight, I'm glad I didn't. She probably would have banished me from the table permanently.

Grasshopper "tobacco spit" on the hands wasn't nearly as problematic as "worm guts" under the fingernails. A quick swipe down the blue jeans and it was gone. Crayfish, meanwhile, weren't especially messy to use, but rather delightfully dangerous to handle. Corralling and impaling one of the crustaceans without serious injury from those snapping pinchers required great care—or so we thought.

As an adult, I realize I never can truly understand what it's like to be a child in today's world. So much changes so quickly because of technology. But when I take a kid fishing, and he or she is more interested in chasing frogs, poking crawdads, or skipping stones than holding a rod and reel, I understand the attraction. I've been there, and I join the fun.

The Pole Truth About Fishing
By Ken Cook

(Ken Cook is managing editor of Fishing Tackle Retailer and a newspaper columnist living in Georgia. He shares his name with a long-time bass pro from Oklahoma.)

"You Get a Line and I'll get a Pole ... and we'll go down to the crawdad hole," read the lyrics of an old folk song. I was 7 years old when I first held a mechanical fishing rod and reel. Pap owned a Pflueger baitcasting reel seated on a four-foot steel rod. Green braided line was wound on the reel and a yellow Hawaiian Wiggler lure was tied on the business end of this fish-catching contraption. Pap liked to walk the banks of Jones Creek and cast under the overhanging branches for "green trout."

Even though Pap owned a rod and reel, he used it infrequently. Our family members were born and bred, true blue, bamboo cane pole fishermen. We rarely fished from a boat because Mama couldn't swim. Our comfort zone was the banks of small streams, rivers, and farm ponds near our southern Mississippi home.

Mama dearly loved to fish; in fact, fishing was her chief interest outside home and family. Though she feared fishing from a john boat, she treasured the trips to Logtown, Mississippi, where bayou backwaters yielded pole-bending fish of various species.

There is still something mystical about a whippy, 10-foot cane pole, rigged with care and precision. I used to watch hypnotically as my father tied monofilament line two feet from the tip, wrapped the knot with black electric tape, wound the line back to the pole's tip, tied a knot at the tip, and wrapped that knot with tape. His methodology ensured the pole would bend rather than break when a "whopper" took the bait.

Pap then stripped line from the spool and carefully snipped it six inches below the butt end of the pole. Like a surgeon preparing to operate, he took from a small paper sack a short-shank bream hook, two tiny lead sinkers, and a small cork. When these items were attached in their proper locations, Pap wound the line down the pole and secured the point of the hook under adhesive tape at the end of the pole.

For cane pole fishing, a tackle box was the small brown paper sack used by the retailer to hold the items you had purchased. Pap kept his "tackle sack" rolled-up and stowed in his left front shirt pocket.

Technological innovations designed to increase fishing success (and tackle sales) now drive the fishing tackle industry and "new" is the operative word that sends us racing to fishing tackle outlets and catalogs to purchase the latest gadgets. Even the lowly bamboo cane pole has not escaped this trend. There are now telescoping fiberglass poles made for bream and crappie fishermen.

Technology aside, there is something therapeutic and nostalgic about rigging a bamboo cane pole the way your father taught you and then settling back in your lawn chair and watching the cork. You owe it to your kids and grandkids to take them fishing and introduce them to low-tech bank fishing with a cane pole.

If this approach doesn't hold their interest, however, there are suitable and acceptable alternatives. The famous Zebco 33 spincasting reel, first introduced in 1952 and still going strong, is a sure-fire solution. If your kids are very young and need additional coaxing, try a Zebco Dora The Explorer or a SpongeBob fishing kit.

The main point of this monologue is to get busy and take your kids and grandkids fishing.

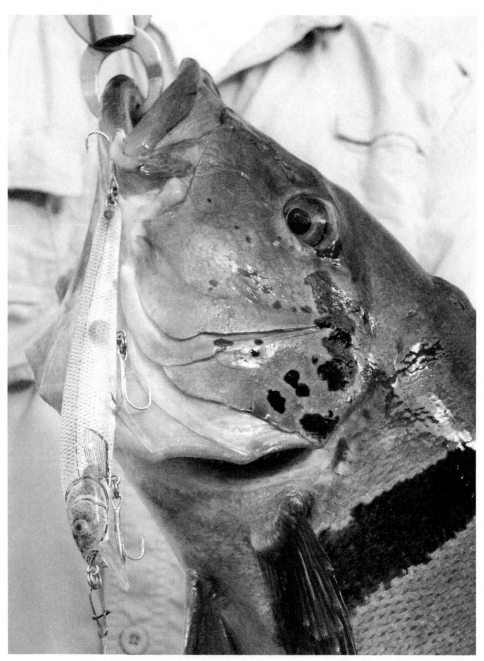

A huge peacock bass is one of the author's legendary fish.

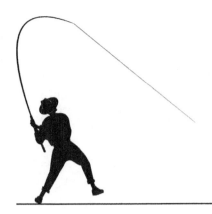

Legendary Fish

A frayed piece of leader owns a place of honor at my desk. It was left to me by a "legendary fish."

That's my own term so I'm not surprised if you haven't heard it before. For me, "legendary fish" is one rung up the ladder from "big," "trophy," and even "fish of a lifetime."

Of course, pursuit of a trophy is one of our prime motivators. Losing a big one fuels the fire in our belly even more. If we can't get the one that got away, we want one even larger.

We replay over and over in our heads how and why we lost those fish. We didn't set the hook hard enough. Our drag was too loose. We didn't hold the rod low enough. And so on and so on. Truth be known, many of our friends and family probably are long-past tired of hearing us recount heart-wrenching tales of those big ones that got away.

For me, a legendary fish is different. Believe it or not, I'm okay with having lost three of those. If I had caught them, would I have been happy? Certainly. Because they were immense fish, each would hold a place of high honor in my memory, and my family and friends would be long-past tired of hearing me recount how I caught them.

So why am I okay with failure? I'm not. I didn't fail. Those fish beat me, pure and simple. With each one, I can think of nothing I could have done differently to bring it to the boat. Call that rationalization if you want. I don't see it that way.

Just having seen and done battle with each for a few seconds is enough for me. In fact, I believe I'm even more pleased with those memories than I would be with heroic photos of me with those brutes.

The first was a rainbow trout. As my party was rafting the Kanektok River in western Alaska, the fish struck a small jig I cast forward from the bow. Instead of streaking downstream, however, it turned and charged toward us. "Big 'bow!' the guide screamed.

And it was. Fifteen pounds, at least. Maybe closer to twenty. I had never seen such a rainbow. It was a wild fish too, hardened by life in a frigid river. Frantically I reeled to catch up with the trout, keeping my rod low and to the side in hopes of discouraging it from going under the raft.

I failed. The 8-pound line lightly kissed the hull as I pushed my rod into the water as far as I could and that tiny bit of friction was enough to break the monofilament.

From start to finish, the "fight" might have lasted five seconds, but those brief moments are forever among my favorites in fishing and high on the list of the many reasons I keep wetting a line.

The second was a peacock bass. Incredibly, the morning had passed on Venezuela's Lake Guri without me getting a single take on a Woodchopper. My friend had caught a couple of small peacocks on a suspending jerkbait, but the day was cloudy and blustery and the fish simply were not cooperative.

Until I threw the topwater to the end of a rocky point. "Grande!" the guide yelled as a huge peacock exploded out of the water with my bait in its mouth and then sped toward deep water. I'll never know for sure, but it appeared to be a 20-pound-plus fish.

With it heading for what I thought was deep, open water, and with me wielding a rod with lots of backbone and 20-pound monofilament line, I was confident this fish would be mine.

Sadly, I was wrong. Submerged brush lay off that rocky point and the big peacock dove right into it. I felt the big head shaking as it wrestled against the pull of my line, and I feared what was coming. I gave the fish slack, hoping it would leave its shelter. It would not.

I tried tightening the line and gently pulling. No luck that way either. I continued to feel the fish moving around, rubbing my line against the brush.

I'm not sure how much time passed. Maybe 30 seconds. Maybe five minutes. However long it took, the line eventually broke. Today, I can look back and recognize the peacock was one of my legendary fish and be happy with that, but then, I was angry. I had fished a half-day for one bite and I had lost the fish—and not just any fish either. It was easily the largest peacock I had ever hooked.

I threw my rod down on the deck, not my proudest moment. As the day passed, I thought about what I could have done or not done to catch that fish. Eventually, I focused on the fact that I had spooled with monofilament instead of 80-pound braid. If I'd been using braid, I told myself, I could have beaten that peacock.

A cooperative 10-pounder eased the pain about mid-afternoon. I began to think more reasonably and was kinder with myself. I had stopped using braid in Brazil, I remembered, after a peacock struck at the boat, buried the braid in the reel, and popped it as if it were kite twine.

Of my three legends, the peacock is the one I come closest to wishing I'd caught. Unlike with other large fish I've lost, however, I'm content with how I handled the fight, as well as why I was using monofilament. I am not happy, though, with how I behaved in the aftermath. Throwing down the rod was petty and childish and could have cost me dearly if it I'd broken it. As my fishing buddy later reminded me, the rod was his.

The third legendary fish was a blue marlin. I've never caught one of those impressive billfish and wasn't even thinking about them on that day off the Pacific coast of Costa Rica.

We were trolling for small yellowfin tuna, using 20-pound spinning gear and spoons. Most of the fish we caught were in the 5- to 10-pound range, perfect for the sashimi we would enjoy that evening.

As anyone who's caught tuna knows, they are fast, hard-fighting fish that stay deep. Suddenly, though, the one I hooked didn't know its place, as it leaped from the water and greyhounded across the top. At first I didn't recognize the contradictory behavior.

Then the captain started yelling from the tower, "Marlin azul! Marlin azul!"

And I saw what was happening. The tuna on the end of my line wasn't trying to get away from me; it was trying to avoid being eaten by a blue marlin.

It failed, and, for a precious few seconds, I was connected to an enormous billfish with tackle never intended for such a battle. As the fish leaped a second time, it slashed its bill violently in protest to being tethered and sliced through the 120-pound monofilament leader, a portion of which now resides at my desk.

Showing multiple frays from the fight, that line, and the memory are enough for me. If by some extraordinary luck I had managed to catch the marlin with a spinning rod and 20-pound line, I would have been proud, of course. But some fish just aren't meant to be caught in a time and manner that we, as anglers, choose. They are the legends, and I'm humbled that I battled three of them.

With any luck, one day I'll chance upon a fourth. All by itself, anticipating such an encounter is reason enough for me to fish.

Why We Fish: The Quiz

*C*omedian Mitch Hedberg had this to say about why we fish: "You know when they have a fishing show on TV? They catch the fish and then let it go. They don't want to eat the fish; they just want to make it late for something."

He makes a good point—from the fish's perspective anyway.

What might fish be late for? I'll refrain from stating the obvious and allow you to answer that yourself, and while you're at it, answer the questions in the quiz below about why you fish. You don't need a No. 2 pencil for this one, and there's no time limit. Heck, you don't even have to write down your answers. Cheating is allowed.

Answer options: Yes, No, Maybe, True, False, Never Thought of That, Are you Serious?

1. I own a garage full of fishing tackle. I have to do something with it.
2. I don't have to wear funny shoes, ice cream-colored shirts, and plaid shorts to go fishing.
3. For my sanity.
4. Ray Scott made me do it.
5. I have to do something with all of those flies I tie.
6. My father taught me.
7. Planning and anticipation make me happy.

8. For the groupies at the tournament weigh-ins.

9. I have worms.

10. We wouldn't have boats if God didn't intend us to fish.

11. I've never had a bad day on the water.

12. The big one could bite on my next cast.

13. For my kids.

14. It brings back memories.

15. I bought a truckload of Vienna sausages.

16. For the sunrises.

17. No one at the end of life ever said, "I wish I had fished less."

Contradicting 'Corps' Beliefs

*I*f not for impoundments built and managed by the U.S. Army Corps of Engineers, waters for fishing—especially bass fishing— would be but a fraction of what they are today. In other words, this federal agency has contributed significantly to why we fish or, more accurately, why we *can* fish.

By extension, tournament fishing, tackle innovation, and all the rest associated with the sport have evolved as they have because of this expanded resource. Consequently, we, as anglers, owe much to the Corps, and therein lies a seeming contradiction that drives many of us to distraction:

These reservoirs were not created for fishing, nor are they managed for fishing. Because they are so critically important for the existence of the sport, many of us simply cannot accept that reality. We can't rid ourselves of the mistaken idea that, when the Corps acts, it is doing so solely to impact fishing in one way or another.

For example, when the Corps lowers the water during or just after the spawn, many of us are certain the move was done either to intentionally damage the fishery and/or to remind anglers who's in charge. The truth is that recreation might be an authorized use on a Corps impoundment, but water storage typically is not allocated for recreation. And that's a crucial difference.

Additionally, a single Corps impoundment is not an independent entity unto itself, especially when it comes to flood control. Reservoirs on a river system are all interrelated in their management.

Consider Table Rock Lake on the White River chain, where more than 13 inches of rain fell within 72 hours during one recent spring, contributing to an historic 21-foot rise.

Beaver Lake is upstream, while Bull Shoals, Norfork, and Greers Ferry are downstream. Between Bull Shoals and Table Rock is Lake Taneycomo, a riverine impoundment not managed by the Corps, but which must be considered in management decisions.

"It's a complicated system," says Greg Oller, Corps manager for Table Rock, who adds that a White River water control plan helps determine when to release and how much, based on storage capacity of the impoundments.

Adding to that complication is the fact that the White is a tributary of the Mississippi, as is the Arkansas. When heavy rains and floods occur, flow down those two waterways must be considered as well in determining releases. Gauging stations help track what's going on.

"From Beaver to Newport (on lower White River) is a lot of uncontrolled area, including the Buffalo River and Crooked Creek," Oller says. "Those elevations can bounce up based on water inflow from rain."

Then there's the heavy rain that poured into Beaver, just as it did to Table Rock. That came barreling down the White River and into Table Rock at 300,000 cubic feet per second. High, muddy water also pushed in from the Kings and James rivers, as the lake rose perilously close to the top of the dam.

By contrast, construction of these impoundments on the White were based on flooding in 1927 and 1945, when peak discharge was 200,000 cubic feet per second.

"A lot of people were upset with the flooding downstream," says the Corps manager, who didn't sleep much during this critical period, "but Table Rock prevented a tremendous amount of damage."

Oller is a fisherman himself and recognizes that these high waters often are good for fisheries, even as they're devastating for homes, towns, and farms in the floodplain. Flooded shorelines provide abundant habitat for fry to feed and avoid predation. "The flood events we had in 2008 and again in 2011 should make these fisheries hot spots for years to years to come," he says.

He adds that the Corps "tries to be sensitive" to fisheries-related issues, but has limited options. "We can't manipulate the water level based on the spawn," he says. "When water is drawn down during that time, it is based on an authorized allocation of water."

As an example, water pulled for hydropower during a dry spring could cause a low-water situation that damages fish reproduction. For fisheries particularly, low water can be more devastating than floods, Oller adds. "You get locked into a drought and that can last for months and even years," he says.

Bottom line, though, is that water is cyclic. There will be droughts. There will be floods. In managing our impoundments during these times, Corps employees must utilize a complicated system based on authorized uses and allocations—not what fishermen want to create optimal fishing conditions.

Fishing together turns buddies into friends.

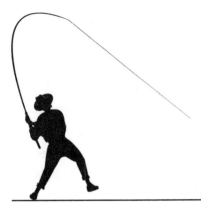

Fishing for a Friend
By Steve Chaconas

(Owner of National Bass Guide Service, Steve Chaconas catches bass and snakeheads on the Potomac River and is a fishing friend of mine.)

My best friend and I didn't share many similarities. He was from a small West Virginia town. I was a world-traveled military brat. He drove a Dodge truck. I cruised in a classic Volvo sports car. He was a concrete finisher. I was a salesman.

When I began dating my wife about 28 years ago, I met her older sister's husband, Dave. With not much in common, we tolerated each other well. At weddings, family reunions, and other visits, we were far from developing a relationship. But bored out of my mind, on the couch, eating and watching TV one day, my idle comment "I'd rather be fishing" started one of the closest friendships I've ever had. Dave picked up on it and expressed interest in taking up fishing again.

From that day 20 years ago, we fished and bonded, bonded and fished. After beginning with casts from the banks of small private farm ponds, we graduated to bigger and bigger fisheries, exploring first with a canoe, then a small plastic boat, and eventually to our present day big bass machines. While our comfort and skills increased, so did our relationship, and we learned that we did have some things in common. We were both left-handed, liked rotisserie chicken and root beer, and didn't like the Dallas Cowboys.

Our dawn to dusk (or much later) fishing escapades were well documented by those who watched us sitting all day, making cast after cast. We were soon dubbed "iron butts," a tribute to our bottomless endurance.

Fishing trips were no longer an adjunct to family gatherings. We planned weekends to fish, while our wives found quality time at the mall, hairdresser, and movie theater. Time with Dave included the hour drive to the lake, fishing 12-plus hours, and the hour return drive.

Not once was the radio on during the time on the road. We always talked. We wondered whether our wives were out of bed yet. We wondered what they were doing at various times of the day. As the day wore on we wondered what they were making for dinner. Mixed in were recounts of fishing days gone by, fish talk of the day, and looking ahead to the next time.

Our conversations allowed me to slow down and smell the fresh air. An avid outdoorsman, Dave pointed out wildlife behavior I had been oblivious to. Even taboo topics, religion and politics, were fair game. We differed on the latter, while finding common ground on the former. About eight years my senior, Dave's perspective and quality character made me a better person. Wherever we went, his low-key demeanor was met with a smile and pleasant greeting. Dave never had to say much; he lived his solid character.

Eventually, we both took on more public, tightly wound professions. Fishing allowed us to unwind. My career was talk radio. Dave took to politics, winning big as a minority party member in his county. No matter whom they ran against Dave, he walked away the winner. After each election we had our traditional post-election fishing trip, allowing Dave to totally relax. We took each day as it came, never having much of an eye on the future.

About ten years ago we discussed retirement as we observed two old guys, fishing and in mild argument. We felt we would be they, someday. Now we were planning for our future together, fishing out our retirement. For the years to follow, we fished no matter the weather. Snow, wind, rain, sun, it didn't matter. Every day was great. Dave always would ask if I was having a good time. We always had a good time.

As well as our plans were laid out, God had another idea for Dave. Just before we were getting ready for a week of Potomac bassing, Dave found out he had cancer. A month later he was gone.

We never really had our last fishing trip, but Dave made an effort to go to the lake and make a few casts.

That last day at the lake, Dave and I had that "final" conversation. There was no doubt this was our last chance to say anything to each other. Weakened by cancer, medication, and loss of appetite, Dave's last words to me were "Thank you for everything." The guy who's given me so much was thanking me!

It started out being about fishing, but soon became about friendship. Time on the water with Dave made me realize there is more to fishing than the fish, the boat, and the lake. It is about yesterday, today, and tomorrow. And it is about relationships, with fishing working its magic.

When Dave died, I lost more than a fishing buddy; I lost a friend.

Chef Philippe Parola says we should eat more carp.
Photo courtesy of Philippe Parola.

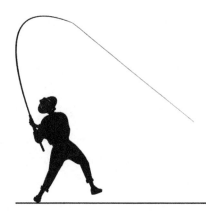

Biting Back

*O*kay, enough is enough.

Down in Louisiana, fear of flying carp is keeping froggers out of the bayous at night.

On Lake Tunica in northern Mississippi, a woman sustained a broken collarbone when she collided with a barrage of silver carp while tubing.

In reporting on the latter, the Natural Resources Defense Council said, "Despite somewhat sensational coverage that implied she was attacked, she wasn't. The fish were doing what comes naturally when startled.

"Her experience is, sadly, not unique. Vast stretches of our waterways are being eliminated from recreational use by the carp's presence. Folks in places like Peoria, Illinois, have long since abandoned recreational activity on the Illinois River for fear of similar incidents."

The feds aren't going to solve this problem. In fact, silver and bighead carp eventually will make their way into the Great Lakes and possibly devastate the sport fishery there because of politics and bureaucratic incompetence.

As with most everything else, the best means of dealing with this expanding invasion is private initiative. Or, as Gary Tilyou, Louisiana

Inland Fisheries administrator advises: "When one jumps in your boat, eat it."

Tilyou is not the only one in Louisiana recommending that solution, which, admittedly, will require considerable corn meal.

"The Asian carp is not just a Great Lakes problem," says Chef Philippe Parola. "Our solution is to break down these delicious invasive fish and mass produce precooked boneless fish fillets for U.S. grocery stores and restaurants.

"This solution will immediately and rapidly remove these invasive fish from our waters."

He adds that commercial harvest of silver and bighead carp will create jobs, boost local economies, "and offer a much cleaner, domestic fish. To date, more than 85 percent of U.S. fish consumption is imported and the majority of these imported fish are contaminated with pollutants or abused with overdoses of sodium for preservation and weight purpose."

Also a recreational angler, Parola is at the forefront of a movement that seeks to control carp, lionfish, wild hogs, and other invasives by popularizing them as food. As global commerce and increased mobility have accelerated these invasions in recent years, this campaign seems as likely as any government intervention to take a bite out of the problem.

Especially if anglers and others will give carp a chance.

"The meat is white. I've eaten it numerous times," says Tilyou. "It's not common carp. That's a different fish."

Parola adds, "The taste is a cross between scallops and crab meat."

Besides buying "silverfin" at the markets and restaurants when it becomes available, anglers can help in other ways. The most obvious way is to keep carp when they jump in the boat, as Tilyou suggests.

Snagging and bowfishing tournaments also can reduce populations and put food on the table, and the field is wide open for figuring out ways to get these filter feeders to bite on baits.

Parola is quick to advise that the carp, once caught, should be bled as quickly as possible to improve the taste, and he acknowledges that bones are abundant. That's why he has focused on marketing items such as gumbo, cream bisque, and fish balls and cakes, as opposed to raw fillets.

Most of us don't even want to think about targeting invasive silverfin and bighead carp. Bass, trout, and walleye are more to our taste, figuratively speaking. Putting the bite on these invaders to diminish their numbers, however—whether we catch them ourselves or buy products made from those caught commercially—could very well make the difference in whether we want to go fishing at all in the future.

Following are recipes developed by Parola for "silverfin:"

Silverfin Fried Strips - 4 servings
    16 strips of silverfin fish (boneless if possible)
    2 eggs
    1 cup of Kleinpeter half & half for eggwash
    1 cup of Louisiana fish fry seasoned flour
    Peckapepper mango sauce for dipping

Preheat fryer at 350. In a bowl, crack 2 eggs, stir well, and then add half & half. Stir well again. Place the strips in eggwash. Coat each strip with seasoned flour. Fry until done. Serve with mango sauce.

Silverfin Cakes - 4 servings
    1 pound of silverfin white meat
    4 ounces of melted unsalted butter
    1 tablespoon of Dijon mustard
    1 tablespoon of lemon juice
    1 whole egg
    1 ounce of crumbled bread
    Seasoning and hot sauce to taste

Poach or steam silverfin meat until fully cooked. Break it up in pieces to remove bones. Place the meat in a mixing bowl. Add butter, mustard, egg, and lemon juice. Mix well and add crumbled bread. Season to taste. Make small cakes, roll in egg wash and seasoned flour, and then fry.

Laissez les bons temps rouler!

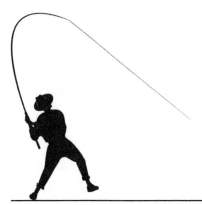

What Might Happen When You Go Fishing

*I*f you're reading this book, you probably don't need a reason to go
fishing, but it never hurts to have a few extras in reserve, in case
you need more justification for your mate, parents, children, boss,
pastor, and/or parole officer.

1.   When you go fishing, you might win the lottery. No kidding.

That's exactly what happened to Stephen and Terri Weaver when
they went fishing down in Arkansas. On their way to the lake they
stopped at a convenience store about 60 miles northeast of Little
Rock to buy a lottery ticket. On their way home, they stopped again
for the same reason.

The first ticket turned out to be a $1 million winner, while the
second netted the Weavers $50,000. They said they would use the
money to pay off debts and invest in their retirement. No mention
was made of buying a new boat, an omission I find difficult to believe.

2.   When you go fishing, you could set a world or state record,
        no matter what species you're pursuing. Here's an interesting
        tidbit the folks at the International Game Fish Association

(IGFA) once shared with me: Sometimes a record-size fish of one species is caught by an angler pursuing another. That's what happened in Texas, when Barry St. Clair caught the state record largemouth (18.18 pounds) while fishing for crappie on Lake Fork.

The IGFA, by the way, is official record holder for both fresh and saltwater species in a variety of categories, including line class and fly fishing. The Freshwater Fishing Hall of Fame also maintains records, as does every state. In addition, many states recognize exceptional catches that aren't necessarily record setters. Two of the most notable are ShareLunker in Texas and TrophyCatch in Florida, both for largemouth bass.

Mostly, you'll receive a certificate or pin to honor your achievement. Depending on the species and your marketing expertise, your record fish could be worth as much as the Weavers' $1 million lottery ticket. The largemouth bass record is one of the most desirable in that regard because of all the endorsements that could be associated with it, from rod and reel to bait and boat.

The horned pout record? Not so much.

3. When you go fishing, you might catch dinner, and that's something you really should consider doing every now and then, especially if you have children who go with you. One of the great joys for a kid is actually eating the fish he or she caught.

Cleaning the fish isn't quite so popular, except for some—usually boys—who enjoy blood and guts. But if you make cleaning and eating an inseparable part of the pact for keeping fish, kids quickly participate.

Keeping fish to eat also is a good way to introduce children to the idea that being an angler includes the responsibility of being an ethical sportsman and conservationist. That means obeying creel and size limits, treating fish respectfully—including those you keep to eat—and keeping waters clean from both trash and pollution to ensure healthy waters and fisheries.

4. When you go fishing, you might be healthier afterward, even if you get skunked, drenched by a downpour, or lose a couple of pints of blood to voracious mosquitoes. I have empirical evidence to prove it happens for me.

For years I insisted fishing is my escape, my way to decompress. I've called it my "brain rinse," a term that not everyone understands, but which I find accurate. Fishing literally washes away my troubles, at least for a while.

In saying all of those things, I had no proof. I just knew the sense of well-being I derived from fishing, both while doing it and afterward. Recently, I haven't fished as much as I usually do, for one reason or another. In early spring, I started feeling pressure in my stomach, and it began making noises like a volcano about to erupt. I also felt jittery and tense.

The doctor confirmed I was suffering from anxiety. And my blood pressure was the highest it's ever been—138/80. That top number is perilously close to being classified as stage one hypertension.

So I went fishing for a few days with my good friend Norm Klayman. We caught fish, saw a rainbow, and generally had a good time. When I returned home, I had my blood pressure checked at the pharmacy. It was 118/76. Couldn't ask for better, especially for someone my age. I'm not saying I can abuse my body, go fishing, and suddenly I'll be healthy again. I am saying fishing is a good way to treat what ails me, both mentally and emotionally.

And I am saying I should be on a regular dosage. So should you. So should we all.

Song writers Gary Shiebler and Larry Robinson know that too, as evidenced by the song, "Doctor's Orders," on the four-CD set of "Papa Was A Fishin' Man," by the World's Greatest Fishing Band:

"Surf fishing south of the border, doctor's orders. You've got to get away.

"Get plenty of rest, use 20-pound test, and see me back in 10 days."

I certainly wouldn't mind winning the lottery with a ticket I purchased on my way to go fishing, and a world record would be nice. I'm sure you feel the same way.

In reality, the odds of doing either are small, but you and I can share the joy of keeping and eating fish with a child. We can improve our mental and emotional health, as well, if only we will make the effort.

Even better, we can do both at the same time.

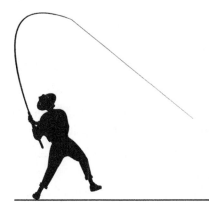

Doing What's Best

*R*emember Largemouth Bass Virus (LMBV)? If you've been a bass angler for more than five years, you certainly do.

Starting in 1995 and for about a decade, it killed fish, especially larger bass, and damaged local economies dependent on recreational fishing. It prompted concern—and even fear—for millions of people that we might be seeing the demise of North America's number one sport fish.

But that isn't what happened. Instead, we discovered the virus would not have catastrophic consequences, although it likely would remain an enduring element in ecosystems, causing sporadic fish kills. Now, here's the rest of the story, the part that you don't know about:

Widespread access and angling restrictions almost certainly would have been imposed in many states across the country had B.A.S.S. not stepped in to stem the panic in 2000.

That's when Conservation Director Bruce Shupp initiated a series of annual workshops on LMBV. At these professionally facilitated events, state, federal, and university scientists and fisheries biologists shared evolving news and research regarding the virus. That invaluable information was then provided to fisheries agencies across the country.

"The situation easily could have gotten out of control," remembers Shupp. "Overreactions were a real possibility, and that would have included stopping tournaments (which came close to happening in at least one state)."

Because of this cooperative process, anglers and resource managers more quickly learned about both the severity and limitations of the virus, as well as how it could be spread and what seemed to trigger it from a dormant virus into a killer disease.

"This was the boldest and best thing we ever did," Shupp adds. "We let the states know what was going on so they wouldn't overreact, and we helped get this thing under control until it dissipated. This was a great example of how to deal publically with a major resource issue."

Shupp is not alone in his assessment of the workshops.

"This was one of the best collaborative processes ever," says Dave Terre, chief of management and research for Inland Fisheries at Texas Parks and Wildlife.

In fact, Terre and three others who attended those events later wrote a paper entitled, "Dealing with Largemouth Bass Virus: Benefits of Multi-sector Collaboration."

"Possibly the greatest benefit was the capability to quickly assemble all available information, provide instantaneous peer review, and develop and disseminate consistent, scientifically valid outreach tools (e.g., fact sheets, news releases)," they wrote.

"Based on declining public concern and fewer sensationalized media releases, these tools apparently were effective. The reality that LMBV was not just a local problem and was being addressed by a regional team also probably helped modulate public concerns."

This prime example of what can be accomplished through cooperation stands in stark contrast to those who prefer conflict and lawsuits as tactics for achieving a goal. That's because making a political statement and/or imposing ideology often is more important to these groups than protecting and/or improving the resource.

Those who want to ban lead fishing tackle profess to care about loons and other waterfowl. Really, they want to stop you from fishing. Why else would they continue pushing for bans when no evidence exists that lead tackle substantially harms wildlife? If they truly cared about loons they would be addressing the real problems: habitat destruction and mortality caused by botulism from eating round gobies, an exotic invasive species.

Those who want to destroy Florida's Rodman Reservoir insist they care about nature and want to restore habitat for fish and wildlife. Yes, it was built during a less enlightened time as part of the ill-advised Cross Florida Barge Canal, a project that was environmentally destructive and never should have been started. However, the reality is that Rodman is as rich and diverse as any natural system, besides being a world-class fishery. Its detractors just want it out because it's manmade.

Those in the Northwest who continue to bash bass because of the demise of salmon and trout—when dams and habitat loss have done the damage—will not accept the reality of altered ecosystems.

"There are some who are dead set against sensible management of any exotic species, no matter how useful they are in providing recreation, funding for conservation agencies, or recruiting young anglers," says Jim Martin, director of the Berkley Conservation Institute. "This issue of management of exotics is a place where sensible conversation about the bigger picture has usually led to a sensible compromise for good management of recreation and native species as well."

Is cooperation and compromise always better than conflict and confrontation? I'm not saying that. In fact, I believe compromise on access issues can be catastrophic for the future of recreational fishing. But when you really care about the well being of a resource, cooperation is the best way to deal with problems. Those who don't come to the table are more concerned with imposing their ideology than they are achieving solutions.

Angling is about spending time together—as well as catching fish.

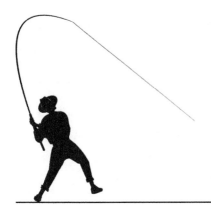

Passing It On
By Ben Leal

(Ben Leal is an outdoor writer and program director for Recycled Fish, a conservation organization.)

The sun rises above the trees. The tires of the boat trailer touch the water. Over the lake, a fine mist makes morning's air visible. After we remove the tie downs, back down the ramp, and shove the boat off the trailer, our day of fishing is about to begin. With the first turns of the motor, my son and I take our seats.

"Dad?" he asks. "Can I help you drive?"

Smiling, I tell him to join me at the motor; we'll share the captain's chair together. Grabbing the tiller handle, I look down at him. "Okay buddy, where to?"

* * * *

If there's one answer to the question of why we fish, that's it. Bonds and relationships are created, whether it's a dad taking his kid for a day on the water or an entire family going out. It's time spent together, and the only distractions are no distractions at all. Distraction is the excitement of a strike that grabs the attention of everyone in the boat. Distraction is an eagle appearing over a tree line that brings conversation to a halt.

Ask an avid angler what got him started, and I'll bet 90 percent will tell you it's the memories shared with dads and granddads. Fishing is not just about catching fish.

As for me, I was an Air Force brat. My dad introduced me to fishing when I was very young. Can't say I remember the first time, but we took many trips together while we were living in South America as part of the U.S. Embassy.

Neusa Lake was about two hours from Bogota, Columbia, where we were stationed, and it was full of fish. We spent our weekends up there, trolling for big brown and rainbow trout, a continent away from our own. My dad would take me and my brother, or we would make it a family outing of six. He shared his fishing wisdom with me, encouraged me when I caught a fish, and laughed with me at the silly things kids do.

My dad's lure of choice back then was the "flatfish." You probably know the one. It's a balsa wood lure that more or less imitates a minnow; he loved to use those lures. Dad out-fished us most days, and if he didn't have the most, he'd catch the biggest.

As we grew older we still found time to fish, taking camping trips to northern New Mexico. We traded our big mountain lake for a small mountain stream, this one also teeming with trout. We'd take short adventure trips to find new areas to fish, but always end up at the same spot.

When I grew up, I followed in my dad's footsteps by way of vocation and enlisted in the U.S. Army. The last summer before I left for Germany, my dad, brother, and I took a trip up to that mountain stream for old time's sake. I still have the pictures of that trip.

Now it's my turn. It's time to pass the torch to my son, but it's more than just teaching him how to fish. It's about creating an everlasting bond between us and providing him with memories he will take with him long after this fisherman makes his last cast. We've spent many hours out on the lake, and each one of those trips is full of memories.

One snowy weekend we went out to do a bit of ice fishing. I set up the shack, drilled a few holes in the ice, and started to fish. But Benny, well, he was more interested in seeing how far he could slide on that frozen lake. "Dad, watch this!" he yelled as he ran toward the ice house. In an instant he'd slip to his side and slide down the ice.

"That was great kiddo," I encouraged him.

"Don't reel in the fish if you catch it, Dad. That's my job."

So he'd slide and I'd hook the fish. Every time I got a feisty fish tugging on my ice rod, he'd come slip-sliding over and reel it in. In my office, I have a photo of my son holding one of "his" fish from that outing.

My son doesn't remember those first outings as much as I do, but there is one he still talks about today. When he was just 7 years old, his mom and I decided it was time to take him on his first Canadian fishing trip. We also took along Brandon, a young friend of ours who was 16. That year was hot. Water temperature at the main lake was high, so we mostly fished early in the morning or late in the day. One day we decided to drive to a nearby lake that was supposed to be extra fishy. The owners of the resort where we were staying said the lake didn't have a lot of big fish, but you could catch a lot of fish. We thought it sounded perfect for the boys.

Shortly after we arrived, we realized this small lake was a perfect body of water. Lots of northern pikes lurked in the reedy shallows, while walleye stacked up along the edges of a large rock formation. The boys caught fish all day long, including some 20-inch walleyes.

After we had our shore lunch, it was my turn to fish with Benny. We cast in a cove, catching mostly northern pike, with most of them "hammer handles."

I was standing in the back of the boat when I heard Benny yell, "Dad, I got another fish!" I told him to go ahead and reel it in and I would help him with it. After a few more minutes, he was still cranking, and his hollering became more insistent. "Dad! I *can't* reel it in anymore!"

I turned to see him with the butt of the rod jammed into his belly, and its tip dipping toward the water. I looked down, and there, hovering just beneath the surface was a walleye—a huge walleye. "Don't move," I said. I dropped my own rod, grabbed the net, and scooped up what would be the fish of a lifetime for most anglers.

After quite a bit of celebration and picture taking, a measurement confirmed my son had landed a 26-inch walleye. Later that day, I bested his by just half an inch. To this day, he still talks about that walleye, the experience, and the fact that I caught a fish just a bit larger than his.

For Brandon this trip would also prove memorable. This was his first Canadian fishing adventure and he'd never hooked a northern pike.

We managed to land quite a few of them, but nothing noteworthy until one early morning. Rigged up with crawler harnesses, we had brought several nice walleye to the boat for our lunch that day. As the morning wore on, Brandon announced he had another hook up. This time, it was a much better fish. After several minutes of fighting, the fish showed itself at the surface as a big northern pike. "Easy on the line, Brandon," I encouraged him. "We don't have metal leaders on." Several tense minutes followed before I scooped it up for him.

"Man, this is awesome!" Brandon said, with a smile beaming from ear to ear. We measured that fish at 32 inches, the largest northern pike caught at the camp that week.

I've spent a lot of time out on the water with this young man who will be 21 soon. He since has bested that pike by 10 inches, but we've also created memories and shared valued lessons out on the water. I hope he will share some of those lessons with his family someday, when it's his turn to pass the torch. The lessons learned on the water don't have to be confined to family; fishing is a great way of mentoring any youngster.

I know I'm not alone in believing the blessings of fishing should be passed on. Some of the greats in our sport shared their experiences with me. One is Jerry McKinnis, whose long-running fishing show, "The Fishing Hole," always ended with "Dedicated to Dad. He always had time to take me fishing." I grew up watching his show. The one thing I remember best is that small dedication at the end of each broadcast.

I asked Jerry about that dedication and what it meant to him. "Fishing creates bonds between sons and fathers. Those are memories that will live on for generations," he said. "My dad and granddad took me fishing and it's something I will never forget."

Kevin VanDam is one of the most successful anglers of all time—the Michael Jordan or Tiger Woods of our sport. As he was making his way to his boat one morning at the Bassmaster Classic, I said, "Kevin, I have quick question for you."

"Sure," he said.

"Who got you started fishing?"

He looked down as if to visualize the moment, and then with a smile on his face said, "My dad. He took me ice fishing. I was three years old." He walked away still carrying the smile my question brought to his face, to launch his boat into the Super Bowl of bass fishing.

Mike Iaconelli is a Bassmaster Classic champion and an Angler of The Year, and one of the most recognized names in our sport. He said his entire family would go fishing together. "I was two years old according to some pictures my mom has," said Iaconelli. "I don't remember those early years of fishing, but I do remember the times we spent as a family. We all grew close in those days, and it's something we share to this day."

I asked recent Bassmaster Classic champion Chris Lane about his start and what his thoughts were. Like KVD, he smiled. "Dad and grandpa took me and my brothers fishing. Back then we didn't have much. Sometimes all we had was a string tied to a stick and a worm on the end of a hook," he said. "We loved it, though, and we shared hotdogs on those early trips."

Now he takes his kids out and enjoys passing on the love for the sport, "and we still share the hot dogs."

Ish Monroe told me his dad took him fishing when he was two years old. "I have pictures of myself holding up some catfish back then," he said. "I still fish with my dad."

A two-time Bassmaster Classic champion, Hank Parker shares his love of the outdoors with two sons in the television show "Hank Parker 3D." He said both his father and grandfather took him fishing. "They weren't as fascinated by it as I was, but that's where I got my start," said Parker. "I was just mesmerized by these fish, and I wanted to know why they would eat this plastic worm. It fascinated me, but it's all because my dad and granddad had the time to take me out fishing as a boy."

It doesn't matter whether the kids we take fishing are our own. When we take a young person with us, the seeds planted often blossom into lifelong passion. Maybe we'll see one of them grow up to be a future Bassmaster Classic champion. More certainly, though, we'll see them develop character through the patience that they learn. We'll see them discover how to slow down by stepping away from screens and into streams. We'll watch them learn the value of nature, why our choices everyday matter, and why we need to protect these places. From the time we invest in them on the water, we'll see them learn to love.

We'll see them become happy, productive members of our family of anglers, eager to pass their love of fishing on to the next generation.

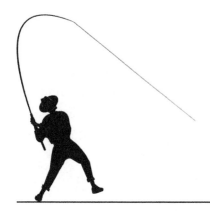

Trip Proud

Years ago, friends and I spent the night at Jack Wingate's Lunker Lodge on Georgia's Lake Seminole.

I didn't sleep well. Instead, I tossed and turned, anticipating the day ahead. Because it was late February, we hoped to find aggressive, pre-spawn bass cruising the shallows. Eventually, anticipation turned to worry, as I feared I'd be too tired to enjoy the day's fishing. At breakfast, I mentioned the night of fitful sleep to my friends, all of them veteran anglers with more experience than I.

"Oh, that," said one. "You were just being *trip proud.*"

Trip proud?

What a great description! Those words perfectly fit what I'd just experienced. And, even better, my friend's understanding revealed I wasn't alone in my suffering. I didn't ask if any of them had been trip proud the previous night. That's because what had occurred didn't seem so negative anymore. Having a name for what happened to me and knowing it was related to something I loved to do suddenly made it all better. I no longer worried about being too tired to enjoy the day's fishing.

In other words, I realized being trip proud is a part of the overall experience, a nocturnal prelude to the actual fishing.

I recalled a summer vacation when I was 10 years old, the first time that I'd been trip proud. Just a few months before, we moved to a house about a block away from a public lake and, with water so close by, I was soon hooked on fishing.

Now, we were visiting my aunt and uncle down on the Texas coast, and he promised to take me saltwater fishing for the first time. All night long I lay on the sofa bed and thought about the coming day. I didn't even know enough to ask questions about how we'd fish and what we would catch, so my imagination had free reign.

Back then, I was too young to worry about a lack of sleep. Instead, I just wanted the night to end so we could go fishing. The most excruciating part was pre-dawn, when the adults stirred in the kitchen, making coffee, frying bacon, and whispering.

Trip proud? You bet.

Fortunately for my mental health, I didn't experience that malady often before I learned it had a name and it wasn't a bad thing. I might have worried myself into an ulcer about something that, when given the proper perspective, is really a celebration of life in much the same as a child anticipates Christmas morning.

In the years following that trip to Lake Seminole, I've been trip proud too many times to count, thanks to the opportunities I've been afforded as a fishing writer. I've been sleepless in Alaska, Belize, Brazil, Canada, Costa Rica, Guatemala, Mexico, Venezuela, and South Africa, as well as some of the best fishing destinations in this country.

What I've learned from these trips, which frequently include five days of fishing, is that being trip proud eventually gives way to blessed exhaustion. By the second or third night, I'm sleeping like a baby.

Since I'm just being trip proud for a day or two instead of having insomnia, I don't worry about being tired enroute to that exhaustion. Cynics might suggest all of this is just rationalization and semantics on my part to justify the sleep deprivation that inevitably accompanies me on an overnight fishing trip.

They're entitled to their opinion, but I suspect those who make such accusations are not fishermen.

Why do I think that? Ask an angler if the night before an eagerly awaited fishing trip isn't a bit like the night before Christmas when he or she was a child. You'll see it's not about losing sleep; it's about being *trip proud*.

Fishing is mystery and anticipation, especially in the early morning mist.

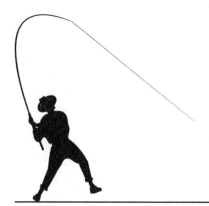

Mystery and More

*M*uch of the pleasure we derive from life comes from mystery — and the exquisite anticipation that accompanies it. What's in that big present under the Christmas tree? Will this next lottery ticket be the big one? Will the Cubs finally win the World Series this year?

For my money, no other pastime comes close to fishing in tapping into that oh, so human pursuit of happiness. Yeah, you can apply the correlation to any sport: Will my next drive be a hole-in-one? Will our doubles team win the tournament? Will I come through with the bases loaded?

But fishing *is* mystery and anticipation: We cast a line in hopes of connecting to an unseen creature in an alien world. Even better, the mystery — the thrill — renews with every cast. Unlike a lottery ticket or slot machine, we don't have to pay for the privilege. This phenomenon that keeps us going back to the water is more motivating as we age and gain experience, I suspect. That's because we become more thoughtful about and appreciative of fishing.

For me, the ultimate in that regard occurs during early mornings on Lake El Salto, a bass lake in the mountains of western Mexico. The sun hasn't yet risen above the mountains to the east, and it's just light enough to tie on a big topwater. Mist shrouds the shoreline shallows, and a ghostly heron remains perched on a flooded fence post, not quite ready to begin its day.

At this time and in this place, I am almost overwhelmed by the mystery of the moment and the anticipation that urges me to cast even before we've stopped the boat. El Salto is a big-bass lake, and I know a monster awaits me somewhere out there. It won't matter if I don't get a bite on the first cast, or even the second or the third. Conditions are perfect. Trophy fish are there, and the strike of a lifetime could come with the next offering, and do you know what heightens anticipation even more? A big blowup and a near-miss from a bass that looks to weigh more than 10 pounds.

One extraordinary morning, that happened to me on consecutive casts to the same spot. Always the optimist, I put the lure there a third time, and this time I hooked the fish that just wouldn't quit. It weighed 12 pounds.

What pleases me most about that memory, though, isn't that I caught, and released, that big bass. It's vicariously enjoying again the anticipation and how it intensified with each cast and each near-miss.

I also can remember feeling almost unbearable anticipation as a child. Mostly it manifested as sleepless nights, with me thinking about going fishing the next day with my friends. But the mystery? Not so much. Kids live more in the moment and eagerly take what comes instead of pondering what might follow. That's why it's so important for adults to allow them to pursue distractions—chase frogs, dig worms, skip rocks—when the fish aren't biting.

My gang always took fishing gear when we went to the water, but if the bluegill and bullheads weren't biting, we found plenty to keep us busy. One day we caught, and then released, 366 bullfrog tadpoles by building little dams to block their escape and then scooping them up with jars. Don't ask me why I remember the number. I just do.

Also, we'd turn over rocks in search of salamanders and spend hours sorting through large gravel in the parking lot, looking for fossils. One of our favorites was catching quarter-size painted turtles in the "moss" that lined the shoreline of a neighborhood lake.

As an adult, I know the moss was actually filamentous alga and an indication that the water was too rich in nutrients, probably because of fertilizer runoff from the surrounding land. As a kid, I just knew it was a great place to see the heads of those pretty little turtles.

We first tried catching them with a long-handled net, but the moss was too thick. So we waded in and grabbed them by hand. Only problem with that strategy was that, early on, we didn't take the time to make certain what we really were grabbing were painted turtles. A couple of water snakes later, we had learned to be more discerning.

Recognizing and acceding to the importance of quick gratification in the kids we take fishing is important if we want them to learn to enjoy the sport just as much as we do. It will keep them going back, where eventually they will learn that each cast renews the mystery.

Also, our acceptance enables us to appreciate the moment with them, whether that moment is catching a fish or chasing a bull frog, and it leads us to relive through our memories the same wonderful adventures we experienced as children.

B.A.S.S. has had a profound influence on every aspect of sport fishing.

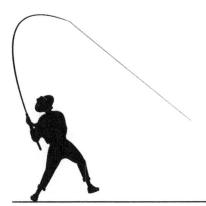

The B.A.S.S. Factor

*I*f you fish, you probably know the name Ray Scott, and maybe you know that he popularized catch-and-release. I doubt you know how profoundly he and his organization have influenced both why and how we fish.

In 1967, Scott staged his first event, the All-American Bass Fishing Tournament at Beaver Lake in Arkansas. A year later he founded the Bass Anglers Sportsman Society (B.A.S.S.), which today has more than 500,000 members and is recognized worldwide for its fisheries conservation efforts, as well as its high-profile bass tournaments.

"If we didn't have B.A.S.S., we would need to create it. It's a tremendous organization," Paul Brouha, former executive director of the American Fisheries Society, told me back in 1998, when B.A.S.S. was celebrating its 30th anniversary.

And Steve Moyer, vice president of government affairs for Trout Unlimited, added, "B.A.S.S. clearly represents Middle America in all of the positive senses. Because of it, Congress and politicians know they cannot do harmful things to environmental laws that Middle America cares about and expect to be successful."

On a more personal level, George Cochran, a two-time Bassmaster Classic winner, told me, "I say my little prayers at night. Not many people can say they do exactly what they want for a living. B.A.S.S. has made that possible for me."

Comments like these reflect the legacy of B.A.S.S. and Scott. They help us see the importance of the organization, both directly and indirectly, for bass fishing in particular and sportfishing in general. As they and the following overview of its contributions attest, if not for B.A.S.S., we would have fewer quality fisheries, fewer anglers, poorer resource agencies, and a sportfishing industry worth far less than its estimated $115 billion annually.

The Anglers

The U.S. Fish and Wildlife Service estimates 40 percent of the nation's nearly 40 million licensed anglers fish specifically for bass. With its tournaments, media support, and savvy publicity department, B.A.S.S. has played no small part in making the black bass the nation's most popular game fish.

"So much of bass fishing's popularity is due to promotion," said Hobson Bryan, a long-time B.A.S.S. member who teaches environmental policy at the University of Alabama. "And B.A.S.S. has done an excellent job of explaining the sport to people who don't know it. I've seen the trend to fishing from ski resorts, for example. Bass fishing has become mainstream news."

Those who decide to try a new pastime, such as bass fishing, usually don't stay at it unless they're successful. Through *Bassmaster Magazine*, *B.A.S.S. Times*, and *The Bassmasters* television show, B.A.S.S. explains to millions of people every month how, when, and where to catch bass.

"Because it's so much easier now to find out what works and what doesn't, young fellows don't have to take nearly as many steps as I did," said Stacey King, a long-time pro from Missouri.

"No doubt about it, B.A.S.S. has helped the average fisherman become much more versatile," fishing legend Bill Dance added. "He can adapt to seasons and to clear or muddy water. He's learned more about fish; how to pattern them and how to use a variety of lures and different depths."

Dance also explained that B.A.S.S. publications have dispelled myths about fishing, such as largemouths are strictly shoreline fish, that bass don't bite in winter or in muddy water, and that sun hurts their eyes.

Through its B.A.S.S. Nation clubs, the organization has provided the vehicle for members to share information and learn about new tackle and techniques from one another, as well as through its publications.

In addition, it has nourished the competitive spirit in many. "Most people like to compete at some level. Tournaments are fun," said Earl Bentz, founder of Triton Boats.

Through B.A.S.S. Nation tournaments, it's even possible for an amateur to win his way to the Bassmaster Classic, compete against the world's best—and win, as the late Bryan Kerchal proved in 1994.

Nation clubs also provide the structure for anglers to do good works for their communities, such as cleaning up lakes, taking kids fishing, and raising money for children's hospitals.

For a few lucky ones, B.A.S.S. has been the means to turn a hobby into a profession.

"It's made our dreams come true," explained Denny Brauer, another Missouri pro. "For the first 30 years of my life, it would have been hard to imagine I could be successful doing this."

Roland Martin added, "Without B.A.S.S., I'd still be a fisherman, but I wouldn't have a TV show. With TV, you get big contracts from sponsors. I owe a tremendous amount to B.A.S.S."

Finally, B.A.S.S. has elevated the image of both professional and amateur bass fishermen and insisted on exemplary behavior for its members.

"People now know we're not all just tobacco-chewing bubba boys," Texas pro Jay Yelas told me in 1998. "And B.A.S.S. is second to none as far as integrity. It's a given that if you want to be a success, you play by the rules. B.A.S.S. has tough tournament directors who often get criticized, but they deserve a lot of credit."

In recognizing their importance as role models, professionals such as Mike Iaconelli and Rick Clunn have often spoken out on behalf of clean water and other environmental issues. Such behavior is right in line with B.A.S.S.' own commitment to preserve and enhance sportfishing.

The Industry

"I remember a B.A.S.S. tournament on (Oklahoma's) Lake Eufaula in the early 1970s, when I was in high school," said Oklahoma fisheries biologist Gene Gilliland. "Roland Martin won it. Afterward, he and Forrest Wood (founder of Ranger Boats) sat out on the dock and talked about how to make livewells better to keep fish alive. The tournament environment, I think, spawned a lot of innovations, especially in boat design and safety features for both the occupants and the fish.

"Maybe they would have shown up anyway eventually," he continued, "but their development was sped up by tournaments, and they became available to the public sooner."

Kill switches, boat hulls, electronics, trolling motors, trailers, and tow vehicles are but a few additional items that owe their current state of development to B.A.S.S. and its professional anglers. Others include specialized rods, reels, baits, lines, tackleboxes, sunglasses, and clothing.

"If my granddaddy could see the equipment today, he wouldn't believe it," Bill Dance said. "He just wouldn't believe what fishing has become."

Roland Martin added, "So many of us now are on design staffs. The tackle and marine industry use us for a lot of different things, but especially research and development."

While B.A.S.S. pros have provided the impetus and expertise, burgeoning numbers of avid bass anglers have proved ready customers for boat, motor, and tackle manufacturers. By the mid

1990s, sportfishing had surpassed Coca-Cola and Dow Chemical on the *Fortune 500* list of top sales producers.

Not surprisingly, B.A.S.S.' contributions are much appreciated by those who make and sell fishing equipment.

"You can't talk about the fishing industry without talking about B.A.S.S.," said Gary Dollahon, who has worked for decades in the public relations portion of the business. "The organization has had a major impact on just about every aspect of the sport over the years, ranging from the evolution of fishing equipment and trends to the creation of fishing celebrities, to the start of many companies in the fishing business today."

With its tournaments and many members, B.A.S.S. also has brought profits to marinas, motels, restaurants, gas stations, and tourist attractions. One study revealed a B.A.S.S. professional tournament brings in more than a half-million dollars directly to a local economy. As the money is re-spent, or "turned over," it provides an economic impact to the community of $1 to $2 million, depending on the length and type of tournament.

Of course, many other organizations have followed B.A.S.S.' lead, staging competitions for bass, walleye, crappie, and other species.

Alabama's Bryan added that the overall economic impact on the national economy by these many tournaments "far exceeds the impacts of specific events."

The Resource

While B.A.S.S. Inc. is a for-profit company, its leaders long ago realized what's good for the sport of fishing is good for the bottom line.

B.A.S.S.' work on behalf of the fisheries resource has been among its most important contributions. We cannot have millions of eager anglers and an ever-growing sportfishing industry without healthy and sustainable fisheries. In 2011 alone, here's what 1,954 B.A.S.S. Nation volunteers did during 12,886 hours of effort:

- 10 tons of trash removed
- 1,662 artificial habitats placed
- 15 miles of roadways cleaned
- $505,700 raised for charities and conservation
- 7,366 acres improved by habitat placement
- 5,000 pounds of invasive grass carp removed
- 350 water willows planted
- 600 bass tagged

"The legacy of B.A.S.S. as an organization is that it has created a more aware fishing constituency that has resulted in better management of habitat and fish populations," said Paul Brouha. "Can you imagine a magazine publishing a photo of a stringer of fish today? A huge shift has occurred."

In 1970, B.A.S.S. founder Ray Scott gained national attention by filing lawsuits against more than 200 polluters and creating Anglers for Clean Water (ACW), a non-profit conservation arm. One of ACW's most important contributions for more than a decade was *Living Waters*, an annual environmental supplement dealing with fishery and water quality issues nationwide.

In 1972, Scott initiated catch-and-release at bass tournaments. Conservation-minded trout anglers had been releasing their fish for decades before that, but it was Scott and B.A.S.S. who generated mass acceptance.

"B.A.S.S. has inspired a lot of young fishermen," Bill Dance said. "I see it all the time in the mail I get. One little boy talked about catching his first big bass and how good it felt to release that fish. Years ago, that little boy never would have released that fish."

Earl Bentz of Triton Boats added that the practice of releasing tournament-caught fish has had a massive ripple effect in salt water. "I remember when they would weigh in blue marlin and throw them in the dump," he said. "Now most of the tournaments are live-release tournaments, and it all began after B.A.S.S. started promoting catch-and-release."

Aside from helping sustain the resource, B.A.S.S.' catch-and-release tournaments—and the additional competitions they have spawned—also provide resource managers with opportunities to do population surveys and sampling studies at little expense.

Also, B.A.S.S. gained conservation clout through the growing popularity of *Bassmaster,* as circulation swelled into the hundreds of thousands by the 1980s.

"Ray Scott called up the vice president (George H. W. Bush) and interceded on behalf of the Wallop-Breaux (W-B) amendments for the Sport Fish Restoration (SFR) Act," said Norville Prosser of the American Sportfishing Association.

Scott and B.A.S.S., Prosser added, were directly responsible for adding an aquatic education component to the program and for ensuring that all of the money gained through excise taxes on tackle and fuel was returned to the states for fisheries management.

"With the amendments, Wallop-Breaux went from $25 million to $102 million annually and OMB (Office of Management and Budget) was trying to say we couldn't spend that much wisely," Prosser said. "Nothing could have been farther from the truth and, fortunately, we had B.A.S.S. on our side."

Biologist Gene Gilliland said that B.A.S.S. provided a voice not for just bass anglers, but all anglers, regarding expansion of the SFR program. "That expansion program was the biggest thing to come along in decades."

To keep an eye on W-B money and help publicize its good works, B.A.S.S. added a full-time national conservation director to its staff in 1991. Throughout that decade, the organization developed cooperative agreements for fisheries conservation with groups such as the U.S. Army Corps of Engineers, U.S. Fish and Wildlife Service, and National Hydropower Association.

Today, Conservation Director Noreen Clough works with sportfishing and conservation groups to make sure that the interests of anglers are voiced in Washington, D.C. She also leads the B.A.S.S. Nation in a campaign to keep discarded plastic baits out of our waterways.

"The most important thing B.A.S.S. has done is raise the consciousness of people about environmental issues," said Bryan. "It's provided an advocacy group and an environmental education we never had before."

In short, if not for B.A.S.S., warmwater fisheries would be without their most outspoken champion, and both anglers and the fishing industry would be much the worse for it.

And if not for B.A.S.S., chances are good that some of us wouldn't even be fishing.

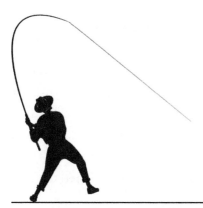

Fishing My Way Through Life
By TChad Montgomery

(Timothy Chad Montgomery is an African-American whose life choices have been guided by his love for fishing and the desire to pass it on. A former competitive angler, he now is a vetrepreneur and works as a master baker.)

*O*ne of the main reasons I fish today is that it helps me recall and preserve fishing memories all the way back to my childhood. Through the years, the reasons I fish have changed.

I grew up with three brothers and three sisters, and I fished to spend time with them. We would wrap the catch in foil with butter, garlic, salt, and pepper. Then we would place it over hot coals. We didn't have a lot growing up; we appreciated fresh fish. Catching fish made me feel like a warrior in a hunter-gatherer sort of way.

My first tackle box came from my Dad. It was green, had one tray, and secured my precious yellow Jitterbug lure. Sometimes, I would keep this lure with me like a pet and then forget it was in my pocket. Sorry, Mom.

Dad taught us everything from how to pick worms by the light of the lantern to how to take panfish and bullhead off the hook without getting finned. I listened. Perhaps, he should have taught me math with this method.

When my father picked up a canoe at an auction, we fished at our local Chittening Pond and I don't ever remember catching anything there. It didn't matter. Watching him row, steer, and study the water's edge taught me to appreciate nature. From that, I learned to fish for the peace it brought me. Fishing kept me living in the present.

Through the years, I've continued to fish with my nieces and nephews, as well as brothers and sisters. We showed the next generation how we grew up, how we survived, and explained to them why we fished.

Also, I got to know my best friend of more than 17 years through fishing. No matter what the weather, it didn't matter; we still fished. Most times it was a race to get the first cast, as it was always the same wagers: $1 for first fish, $1 most, and $1 biggest. We ended up with matching hook tattoos.

Years later, I saw *Bassmasters* on TV. I wanted to set the hook that way and hear Mr. Ray Scott announce my name on stage with my winning tournament weight. I still imitate him doing this.

I went from fishing to catching and I was blessed with generous sponsors who allowed me to compete in nationwide tournaments. I was even fortunate enough to be a guest on my favorite fishing show, "One more cast with Shaw Grigsby."

I enjoyed a nice taste of tournament bass fishing, and I felt the reason I fished was changing again. I wanted everyone to have a chance to experience fishing. I got a job as a sporting goods manager, began speaking at seminars and fishing clubs, and founded a "Fishingfunshop" at New York's Ithaca Youth Bureau. This workshop taught parents who didn't know much about fishing how to take their children fishing. It since has expanded into two workshops and has been an annual event for more than 10 years.

My best friend and I hosted a weekend youth event sponsored by Capital District Youth for Christ. We camped out with more than a dozen kids and the next day we toured Morrisville State College. After a night in the dorms, we met my tournament friends in their bass boats along with the president of the college, Dr. Ray Cross, for a fishing tournament, weigh-in ceremony and picnic. When I recall the smiles, it's easy to see why we fish.

After leaving retail management, I worked with incarcerated youths in a secured facility. Wouldn't you know they had a small pond on the grounds and a large farm pond next door? I got permission to take the honor-roll-type residents fishing as a reward for good behavior. There was a high urban population and more than 80 percent had never been fishing. As behavior improved, interest in going fishing grew. I contacted my fishing sponsors and soon had enough gear for more than 50 residents and permission to take them off state-facility property for a day and night of fishing and camping at the farm across the road. Their smiles and laughter will never be forgotten.

Last month, I fished with my 85-year-old father on his 7-acre pond in southeastern Georgia. The last time we fished together, he set his rod against a tree, and then went to get something from the house. When he returned, he discovered a fish had taken off with everything. This trip began with a new rod and reel combo for my dad.

I taught Dad how to use a soft jerkbait and he caught six fish to my one. He took a picture of mine with his new smart phone and talked about how far technology and fishing rods and reels have come since we began fishing so many years ago. Dad cleaned the fish; I wrapped them in foil, added butter, garlic, salt and pepper, and placed them on the coals. We laughed about losing fish at the boat and places we want to fish again.

For whatever reason you fish, it is time well spent. It is grounding for me. It can take me back to every fishing memory, and each new trip provides new ones. Fishing awakens my competitive side. It challenges my inner survivor instincts, and most of all, it reminds me that life can change at any moment, with one bite.

That's why I fish.

Teaching someone to fish makes the world a better place.

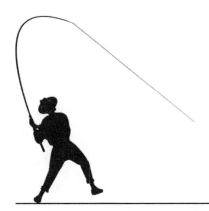

Saluting Anglers

- May you never break a rod in a car door or ceiling fan.
- May you always catch fish—but not too many or too often.
- May your trebles rarely get tangled.
- May you always believe a big one is possible on your next cast.
- May all your backlashes be little ones.
- May you always cherish the joy that fishing brought you as a child.
- May you never get a hole in the seat of your rain pants.
- May you make the world a better place by teaching someone to fish.
- May you never run out of your favorite lure.
- May you never feel too old to get up early to go fishing.
- May ethanol-based fuel be banished to the trash heap of bad ideas.
- May you not miss the rainbow because you are too busy catching a limit.
- May Asian carp never invade your fishery.
- May you have at least one day of fishing so good that no one believes you.
- May you know the peace a day on the water brings all throughout the New Year.

Eating what we catch is but one of the pleasures we derive from fishing.

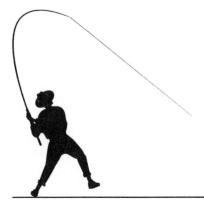

Food for Thought

Something basic draws us to fishing when we're young, I believe. It is the "hunter/gatherer" imperative, passed on from generation to generation as instinct or maybe through our DNA. I'm a fisherman, not a scientist, so to delve deeper into what I'm talking about would be pseudo-intellectual at best.

But you know what I mean: our species survived eons ago by hunting and gathering food. Not doing so would have meant death by starvation. Despite the passage of years, we have retained at least a semblance of that need, no matter how comfortable our existence is today.

When a rod is placed in a child's hands, a spark ignites desire, especially upon catching that first fish. If you've ever taken a youngster fishing, you know what I'm talking about. Inevitably, his first words as he admires his catch are, "Can we keep it?"

Certainly, some anglers continue down that path as they age. They keep their catch for food either because they need to or want to. Others become more introspective in their enjoyment of angling, preferring to focus on the mental, emotional, and social value of a day on the water.

On the other hand, many young anglers quickly learn the catch-and-release ethic and direct their desire from "hunt and gather" into competitive fishing. Fish are still collected and brought back to be admired by the fisherman's friends and family, but instead of being roasted over a fire, they're entered into a competition with money and prizes. Then they are released.

For some of those, the idea of killing and eating a fish is an abomination. I speak from experience. Years ago, a friend of mine from South Africa came to the United States to fish in a tournament. In his country, the bass is an introduced fish, and anglers there learned everything they know about catching it from reading *Bassmaster Magazine* and the related publications it has spawned. Catch-and-release, of course, has been an integral part of that education.

If that's all you've ever known, it's all you ever do. Thus, when a fishing buddy and I took my friend fishing for fun and we kept some bass for the table, he was mortified. He stood with mouth agape as we cleaned them. He insisted he would not even taste them, but when he saw how inviting cooked fish looked and he smelled its delicious aroma, he relented. In fact, he went two plates past relented.

"You can never tell anyone that I did this," he said as he finished his last bite.

That's an extreme case, but it is indicative of where we are with catch-and-release. Many anglers, especially those who pursue bass and trout, would never think of keeping fish to eat. In fact, their refusal complicates management of some fisheries, where harvesting the abundant smaller fish would be beneficial.

Me? I'm still an unapologetic hunter/gatherer, although I'm selective about what I keep and from what waters I keep them. Mostly I keep 1- to 3-pound largemouth and spotted bass from Bull Shoals Lake, a deep, clear impoundment on the Missouri-Arkansas border, or I harvest 10- to 12-inch bass from the small, spring-fed lake behind my house. When they're of legal size, I always keep walleye, and if I catch enough of them, I'll keep crappie.

When my mother was alive, I'd keep catfish for her. In fact, I earned my stripes as a hunter/gatherer doing just that.

I don't remember the first fish I caught. Probably it was a small bluegill or green sunfish. But I do remember the first species I learned to catch consistently—the bullhead catfish. Suddenly, there I was, a 10-year-old bringing home food for the family. I was busting with pride.

Of course, I didn't know many catfish anglers consider the bullhead a disreputable cousin of more desirable blue, channel, and flathead catfish. And I don't know that I would have cared. I was catching fish and my family was eating them!

After I cleaned them. Mr. Wilson, our next door neighbor, taught me to do that. My most vivid memory from that experience isn't struggling to part the head from the body or pulling the slimy skin from the flesh. It's finding rusty hooks in the bellies of those hardy, little bullheads that probably weighed three-fourths of a pound to 2 pounds.

From there, I graduated to keeping bass, and as a teenager I can remember wanting nothing more than to catch a limit. Back then it was 10 or 15; I don't remember which. But it didn't matter. I never made it. Until I was 18, the highlight was catching three 3-pounders with an adult neighbor who took me fishing in a boat for the first time.

Right on through college I kept fish to eat. In fact, catfish, bass, and frog legs helped keep my wife and me from starving during graduate school.

As someone who was mostly self-taught about fishing, I was late to learn about catch-and-release, which B.A.S.S. founder Ray Scott popularized in the early 1970s. Eventually, I, too, became a disciple, but I was not, and have not become the zealot my friend from South Africa was before I corrupted him.

Catch-and-release is a good thing, no question; so is keeping a few fish for the table now and then, both for the sustenance it provides and to honor our hunter/gatherer ancestors whose perseverance gave us life.

Having your boat ready to go when you back down the ramp
is one way of honoring our heritage.

Honoring Our Heritage

We fish mostly because of the personal gratification fishing provides: We catch fish. We spend quality time with friends and family. We relax. We compete.

But as we do all of that, whether we realize it or not, we also fish to sustain a tradition and honor our heritage. We do this by passing on a sportsmanship code of ethics and etiquette to our children that will make them not only better anglers, but better people. That code of ethics is especially important today, as our society becomes even more urbanized, with a growing number of people who know little about nature and the outdoors. These folks judge the value of recreational fishing by how they see us behave on the water.

In general, angling etiquette is a code of courtesy that shows consideration for others and, in doing so, encourages ethical behavior. Angling etiquette is visible through acts such as yielding to the boat on the right, leaving other fishermen plenty of room, and giving way to a smaller, slower craft cutting across your bow.

But what, exactly, is ethical behavior?

Some say ethics are what we do when no one is looking. Others say ethics are another way of expressing the Golden Rule: "Do unto others as you would have them do unto you." I believe ethics are a way of showing respect for ourselves, other anglers, the water we're fishing on, and the fish we're catching. For example, an ethical angler doesn't crowd into another's water. If he's fishing near a private dock, he's especially careful not to damage property with his bait and line. He handles fish with care and releases them gently into the water instead of tossing them back like discarded trash.

"Your ethics are the rules or values you use to help choose behavior that's fair to others and to yourself," says Texas Parks and Wildlife Department (TPWD). "We practice ethical behavior when we do the right thing, even when we think we won't be caught or punished for our behavior."

When trying to decide whether our behavior will be ethical, says TPWD, we should consider these questions: Is it legal? Would it be good if everyone did it? Would it make you proud of yourself?

Also, we shouldn't allow someone's questionable behavior to influence our judgment. In other words, two wrongs don't make a right.

Sometimes, actions that seem wrong to us aren't viewed that way by others, especially non-anglers. Water skiers and jet skiers are notorious for speeding between fishermen and the shore. Is that thoughtless behavior? Certainly, but are they being intentionally offensive? Not necessarily. They may not understand how fishing works, nor is it a priority for them to pay attention to such things.

As fishermen, we do know that motoring between an angler and a nearby shoreline is poor etiquette and possibly unethical if it harms his fishing. The following actions reflect proper etiquette and ethical behavior by anglers:

- Honor another's trust. If someone shares with you his secret spot, don't tell anyone about it, no matter how tempted you may be.
- Whether in a boat or on shore, don't cast your line across another's or into "his water." Doing so not only is unethical but could result in a tangled mess that keeps both of you from fishing.

- Understand and follow fishing and boating regulations. Obeying the law is not only ethical—it also keeps you from paying fines and possibly even going to jail and/or having your fishing privileges revoked.

- Handle fish gently. Don't suspend them out of the water with fishing line. Don't touch the gills. After you net or lip them, don't allow them to flop around on shore or in the bottom of the boat. If a fish "swallows" the hook, cut off the line at the eye and leave it in.

- Never keep fish just to show off. You should be prepared to clean and eat any fish you take home.

- Have your boat ready to go before you back it down the ramp. When you take it out, move quickly out of the way so others can use the launch area.

- Help with loading, unloading, and cleaning the boat.

- Take live bait home with you or dispose of it well away from the water instead of dumping it into the lake. Be certain your boat and trailer don't carry any uninvited hitchhikers, such as nuisance plants or zebra mussels.

- Don't move fish of any kind from one water body to another. In addition to being unethical and illegal, it could do irreversible damage to a fishery you were trying to improve.

- Always ask permission before crossing private property or fishing a pond or stream on private property.

- If you're wading, try to avoid trampling aquatic vegetation. Enter and leave the water at places where the banks are low or at gravel bars, so you'll do less damage to the shorelines.

- If you're fishing on private land and keeping fish, offer to share your catch with the landowner.

- Leave an area just as clean as you found it. And especially never discard line or soft plastic baits. Even better, pick up the trash left behind by others. Littering, of course, is against the law. Picking it up shows respect for the resource.

- Avoid spills and never dump pollutants, such as gas and oil, into the water.
- Share your knowledge and enjoyment of the sport by taking others fishing.
- Always promote angling ethics and etiquette through your own behavior,

Be especially mindful of your actions when you fish with children. You're teaching by example; your behavior determines not only what people think of anglers today, but the opinion of coming generations as well. In other words, the future of fishing depends on it.

The Proof Is in the Popper

With cool days already here and fall coming officially this weekend, I fondly remember an October fishing trip to a farm pond when I was 15. I'll never forget that day, one of many filed away in my brain with angling as its focus. One truism for anglers everywhere, I believe, is that we fish as much for the fond memories we accumulate as we do for the critters we catch—or hope to catch.

When I was 8 years old, I caught my first fish on bacon. I don't remember why I decided to use a breakfast meat, but bluegills and bullheads seemed to like it—as well as a dog or two that put a mighty strain on my cane pole. (How a gang of kids removed a hook from the snout an angry dachshund is a story to save for another time.)

From bacon I graduated to worms, my bait of choice for most of my childhood. I found the wigglers by turning over rotten logs, discarded tires, and even cow patties in a nearby pasture. Of course, the poop had to be aged to just the right texture to attract the critters. I turned over many that weren't.

Although I fished exclusively with worms for years, I carried a couple of "lures" in my green, single-tray tackle box. One of them was a knockoff Bass Oreno and the other an inline spinner. They came with a fishing kit I bought through an advertisement in the back of a comic book.

But I didn't catch a bass on artificial bait until I discovered the plastic worm on a propeller rig. Black, purple, and brown colors seemed to work equally well. They were my first "confidence" baits. When I compare that gaudy contraption to the plastics in "natural shades" we so subtly rig today to make them appear lifelike, I have to wonder if we aren't overthinking our strategies for catching fish. The exploding popularity of the Alabama rig, which is really just a worm harness on steroids, bolsters my belief that we are. Still, this evolution, this constant search for a better bait, adds to the fun of fishing.

My success with a propeller worm prompted my own evolution, inspiring me to consider using more baits I didn't dig up or take from the meat container in the refrigerator when my mother wasn't looking. Using money I made from babysitting, cutting weeds, and cleaning boats, I bought a yellow Hula Popper, an orange, jointed Inch Minnow, and a Shannon Twin Spin. I don't remember why I decided on those three or why I picked yellow and orange for the hard plastics. Perhaps those two colors were my only choices in the sporting goods store where my father took me.

I never caught a fish on the Twin Spin—and still haven't. Of course, I haven't fished with it much either. The Inch Minnow, however, proved a great bait for catching bluegills, green sunfish, and even small bass in farm ponds.

But the Hula Popper. Wow! I have no doubt topwater fishing remains my favorite method of catching bass today because of what happened on that memorable October afternoon. In fact, fishing friends would tell you I'm irrationally addicted to the surface bite and the adrenaline rush that accompanies an aggressive take. For many of them, enjoyment comes from using the most effective bait to actually put fish in the boat. For me, it's about teasing a fish into a visual strike. Landing the fish is secondary.

I wasn't thinking about all that when I cast the popper nearly all the way across Turner's pond. The water was flat calm. I had already caught a 1-pound bass on my fake Bass Oreno and was basking in the glory of the fish I'd tethered in the shallows on my rope stringer. Truth be told, I was focused more on what I'd just caught than what I might catch next.

That's why I didn't pay much attention to the cast or the presentation. Plus, I knew next to nothing about fishing a topwater. Based on years of experience since and what I learned from the pros, if I were to throw that bait on still water 1 today, I would probably twitch it, or at most give it a gentle "plop."

But I had nothing to guide me in proper technique that fall day, and since the bait was a "popper," I popped it. In fact, I popped it as hard as I possibly could, sending ripples all across the pond.

As the pond returned to a glasslike state following my second pop, water under the lure exploded, and I was suddenly tied fast to the biggest bass I'd ever hooked. Of course, it wasn't large enough to pull drag on my Johnson Century spincast reel, but at 3 pounds, it was a trophy in my eyes as I dragged it up on the bank. My heart nearly leaped out of my chest at the sight of that fish, and after placing it on my stringer with the smaller bass, I looked down to see my hands still shaking.

In the decades since, I've caught thousands of bass larger than the one I caught at Turner's pond that fall day, including more than a dozen that weighed 10 pounds or more. I've caught some of those lunkers on big, loud surface baits—often to the stunned surprise of guides and fishing buddies.

But I've never caught one that excited me more than that 3-pounder. In honor of that, I've kept the old yellow Arbogast Hula Popper as one of my most treasured keepsakes. When fall comes around each year, I always think of that special day.

This big bonefish still found the jig, despite a poor cast.

A Fisherman's Thanksgiving Prayer

*F*or the following I am thankful:

- The fondness of bass for topwater lures.
- The rainbows I've seen because I got up early to go fishing.
- The opportunities I've had to fish with friends all over the world and catch all kinds of fish.
- The 10-pound bass I've caught—and those that got away.
- Cold margaritas after a day on the water in Mexico.
- Bluegill too big for me to hold with one hand.
- The catfish, the bowfin, the musky, and the northern pike that hit my bass baits.
- The big bonefish that found my offering, even though my cast was way off target.
- Sailfish that greyhound and tuna that dig deep.
- Sashimi from the yellowfin I caught just a few hours before.
- Thousands of dolphins swimming alongside the boat.
- The good people I've met and the friendships I've made because of fishing.

- River fishing on summer nights for catfish, while listening to the baseball game.
- Bats chasing insects all around the boat under a full moon.
- The unexpected shower from a huge peacock bass that struck right at the boat.
- The delicate take of a tiny dry fly by a big rainbow—just before all hell breaks loose.
- The headshake of a big walleye following the hookset.
- Seeing the joy a child derives from his first fish.
- The power of fishing to bring us together, no matter how polarized we are politically.

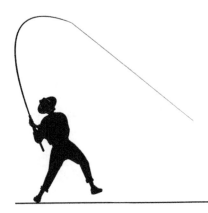

Getting Bit

*F*ishermen talk all the time about "getting bit."

But they aren't getting bit in the way you might think. Fish, you see, don't bite, except for some notable exceptions, including piranhas and sharks. Rather, they swallow their food whole. Even such toothy critters as walleye and northern pike grab and gulp.

Anglers do "get bit" by a myriad of creatures in the outdoors. That doesn't keep us from fishing, but it certainly makes for some uncomfortable hours, days, or even weeks in the aftermath of being a bug buffet. I speak from experience.

Black flies, horse flies, deer flies, gnats, ticks, chiggers, mosquitoes, spiders, fire ants, and even a water snake with a bad attitude have partaken of my flesh over the years, and my apologies to any arthropods I might have inadvertently forgotten.

Top honors go to the tick that bit me sometime around 1990. It gave me Lyme Disease. At the time I was diagnosed, no cases had yet been reported in Missouri, where I live, so I suspect I contracted it during a fishing trip in some other state. The doctor who checked my blood during an outdoor writers conference told me I should have a more specific test to confirm the positive reading was from the tick-borne illness and not a sexually transmitted disease.

Now, I knew I didn't have an STD. Still, I'm one to follow doctor's orders so I marched myself into the county health department and told the nurses I needed a blood test to confirm I did not have a venereal disease. "You see," I said, "I took a test that said I have either Lyme Disease or an STD, and I know I don't have an STD and I'm outside a lot and I've been bitten by a lot of ticks and . . ."

On and on I rambled, trying to explain I was piscatorial instead of promiscuous. The three of them probably didn't smirk, but that's the way I remember it. That was the worst part of my diagnosis, especially considering I've never exhibited any of the symptoms that often accompany Lyme Disease.

I certainly am lucky in that regard, for I've been bitten by dozens of ticks. I get more ticks than my dog—than most anyone's dog. In fact, I determine the arrival of spring by my first bite, rather than by whether the groundhog sees its shadow.

You haven't lived until you stumble into a nest of "seed" ticks— each about the size of the head of a pin—looking for their first blood meal. I've done that a couple of times, which required long, hot showers as I scrapped fingernails over every inch of bare flesh to remove the parasites before they attached themselves.

Like ticks, chiggers—or as they say in the South, "red bugs"— also strike early. Fortunately, my body seems to quickly build up a resistance to the mighty mites with an appetite for blood. In March, a chigger bite will itch for a couple of weeks; by early summer, it's no more irritating than a mosquito bite.

For me, mosquitoes are mostly an "in the moment" type of plague since the after-effects of their bites don't remain more than hour or two. I have been "in the moment" a few times, from the Northwest Territories in Canada to the Florida Everglades. During a fishing trip to Great Slave Lake, we actually dove into the icy water to escape. The only flaw with that plan was that the blood suckers were waiting for us to surface, an obvious certainty we somehow overlooked when we decided to shuck our clothes and take the plunge.

I also credit mosquitoes with the most frightening moment I've experienced in the woods. Close encounters with bears, wolves, and even mountain lions take a back seat to what I heard coming at us as we relaxed inside the screened porch of a cabin, following a day of fishing on a New Brunswick lake. It began innocently enough as a soft murmur, but in seconds escalated into an ear-splitting whine as a horde of mosquitoes—drawn by our body heat—descended on the cabin. I swear I saw the screens vibrating and felt the floor shaking as they tried to get in.

As much as I needed to, I did not visit the outhouse that night.

By this time, it should be obvious that insects love me. They really do. Repellent is just like a honey glaze for them when it's on my flesh. Friends invite me fishing just so the bugs will be attracted to me instead of them.

But the snake. Well, that's another story. I deserved that one. That's the way it usually is with snakes, too. They're minding their own business and someone comes along and tries to spoil their day. In my defense, I was only nine or ten years old, and the banded water snake did have a fish in its mouth.

"No way can it bite me," I thought as I reached for it.

Wrong. In the blink of an eye, it somehow spit out the fish and latched onto my finger. The saving grace for me was that I could identify snakes, even at that age. I instantly knew I'd been stupid, but at least not fatally so. The scratch marks were easy to explain away, especially compared to the frozen blue jeans I acquired when my friends and I decided to try fishing on a creek's too thin ice. "Blackberry bushes," I told my mother.

Still and all, as much as I've been "bit" over the years while fishing— and not by fish—those bites are a small price to pay for the pleasure of spending time near the water with a rod in my hand. I always remain "itching" to go again, even though I know that mosquitoes, chiggers, ticks, and all the rest are out there, just waiting for me.

The fishing trips we take as adults often take us back
in time to the angling adventures we had as children.

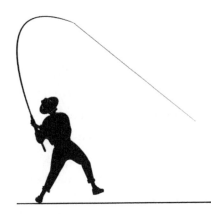

Time Travel

I fish almost exclusively with artificial baits for bass and other game fish. Once a year, however, I dig a batch of worms, clean the dust off my catfish gear, pack some hotdogs and marshmallows, and spend the night tightlining for catfish on a lake or river. In recent years, mostly I go down to the little lake behind my house. No chance of catching flatheads there, but in my mature years, watching moonlight dance on the still water more than makes up for that. It doesn't hurt either that the channel catfish are usually cooperative.

I never thought much about why I was doing this until the latest trip. I was alone for a change and watching the yellow flames of my campfire burn into blue when, suddenly, I felt transported. Mostly, we fish to be in the *now*, to fully engage in an always pleasant and sometimes exciting pastime that takes us away from the nine to five world.

Once in awhile, though, fishing takes us to *then*. Something—the weather, a bait, the day's success, an idle comment—flips a synaptic switch and suddenly we're reliving a day of fishing from our past.

As we grow older, we experience more and more of this time travel. Mostly it's unintentional and just happens. While sitting before the fire that night, I realized I'd been taking these annual trips mostly because they evoke pleasant memories of similar trips

I enjoyed with friends when I was younger. I remembered when we decided to not take food and, instead, eat what we caught. We caught an eel. Fortunately, only two of us were on this Florida river float trip and the eel was a big one, although not big enough, as it turned out. Fried in corn meal, the firm, white flesh of the fish was as good as any we'd ever had eaten. Possibly, near starvation clouded our judgment regarding the taste as we picked the bones clean.

Cleaning an eel, however, is a chore I would never repeat—no matter how good they taste. My greatest regret is that we didn't have cell phones with video capabilities back then. Our bumbling attempts to skin the long, slimy fish were worthy of a YouTube posting.

While roasting a hot dog, I remembered when Leonard broke his rod setting the hook on what was probably a big catfish. Holding the line in our bare hands, we could feel the fish shaking its head out there in the black water, beyond our lantern light. We waded out as far as we dared. For some reason, it didn't bolt downstream in the fast current, and for what seemed like hours, we tried to finesse it into the shallows. Like an irritating mosquito that keeps buzzing in your ear, Gary contented himself with offering sage advice from his relaxed position on the gravel beach.

We had no chance of landing this massive mystery fish and eventually the line parted. We waded ashore, hands rubbed raw by the monofilament.

Another "fish of a lifetime" escaped when we fished above a dam, instead of below, as we usually did. On a black, moonless night, Jerry guided what we guessed was a big catfish out of deep water, and I headed down to the water's edge with a lantern and a landing net. In the wash of light, the fish that had seemed almost somnambulant suddenly awakened and all hell broke loose. Before I could even lower the net, I was drenched by a long, wide body with a broad flat head. It then sped toward deep water and I could hear line burning off Jerry's reel.

"You'd better tighten the drag," I yelled.

"This reel doesn't have one," he screamed back, just moments before I heard the line pop, followed by a long list of expletives.

I also remembered when Gary volunteered to cook breakfast while the rest of us fished. A half hour later, I walked up to find out why he was taking so long. After frying a pound of bacon in the skillet, he was trying to cook the eggs without pouring out any of the grease. It was taking awhile.

We called his eggs "catcher's mitts," but we ate them. As teenage boys, we were so hungry we would have eaten real catcher's mitts at that point, but we never again allowed Gary to cook during our fishing trips.

I remembered nights along the Mississippi River when we believed the wakes from barges turned on the fish, and I remembered an incredible bite during a downpour on the Big River. We were drenched to the skin, yet we felt no discomfort as the flatheads and channels gobbled our nightcrawlers. Even thunder and lightning couldn't chase us away, but rising water finally did.

I remembered bolting up in shock and pain when an ash from the campfire settled on my bare arm as I slept. We put pork and beans juice on the burn. I wouldn't recommend that as a treatment. As a kid who lived to fish, I convinced myself , and my friends, that it eased the pain enough so we didn't have to cut short our trip. I still have the scar.

I remembered when a fish pulled in my rod and reel and, before I could take off my shoes, Chris dived in fully clothed. He retrieved the rod and I reeled in a 3-pound carp. We always preferred catfish to carp because we wanted to take home fish for the table, but fast biting, hard fighting carp provided welcome excitement from time to time, especially when they tried to steal our tackle. Bluegill, buffalo, drum, white bass, walleye, and turtles offered variety as well, although I can't say we welcomed attention from the latter, particularly the big snappers. No one lost a finger, but we came close, as one of us would invariably forget just how long their necks are.

I remembered a more recent trip when Jesse, my Little Brother, and I lay on our backs and watched meteor showers. I don't recall whether we caught anything, but sharing the light show with a young angler as we talked about life provided a memory I'll never forget.

Yes, we enjoy the *now* when we fish, but as we grow older we learn to also take pleasure in *then*. I'm hopeful that our night together watching the meteors will someday be one of those *then* times for Jesse.

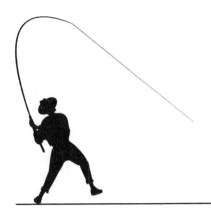

A History Lesson

*D*espite objections from many of the state's anglers, New York recently decided to allow the sale of black bass in markets and restaurants. The regulation stipulates they must be hatchery-raised, but the words of Seth Gordon, the first conservation director for the Izaak Walton League (IWL), serve as a chilling reminder of what once was and what could again be when we don't learn from history.

"So long as there is a legal market anywhere, you may bank on it that thousands of pounds of illegally caught bass will be sold," he said during IWL's all but forgotten campaign during the 1920s to save black bass from decimation by commercial harvest.

Well into the 20th century, black bass were commercial, as well as sport fish. Even as government agencies stocked fish anywhere and everywhere and closed seasons limited sport fishing, commercial fishermen harvested largemouth and smallmouth bass with pound and fyke nets, as well as other means, for sale in the fish markets of many cities.

"Eulogy on the Black Bass" read the headline in a 1927 issue of *Forest and Stream*. A headline in 1930 screamed, "Defrauding Ten Million Anglers." In the latter article, Edward Kemper slammed the Bureau of Fisheries for "overseeing the slaughter of millions and millions of black bass" and he included a "role of dishonor," naming ten states that continued to allow sale of bass in markets.

The Izaak Walton League was the prime mover for passage of the Black Bass Act of 1926, which was introduced into Congress by Rep. Harry Hawes of Missouri. As the law prohibited shipment of bass across state lines, IWL also worked within those states to outlaw commercial harvest.

I learned about this little known chapter in bass history from Jim Long, assistant unit leader of the Oklahoma Cooperative Fish and Wildlife Research Unit at Oklahoma State University. He came across this and other long forgotten information as he prepared a presentation on the history of black bass management for a Black Bass Diversity Symposium at a Southern Division Meeting of the American Fisheries Society.

"I've read some histories of fisheries, but I've never seen one for black bass," he told me. "I wanted original newspaper clippings, not third-hand accounts, and data bases made that possible," he said.

Pouring through archives, Long found a headline from the 1920s that proclaimed, "Hoover Laments Decline of Fishing." He discovered that the New York Times listed black bass regulations during the 1870s. "That's something you don't see today," he said.

As he divided his search into major time periods, starting with the 1800s, what surprised Long the most were the influential roles played by the IWL and, before that, by Dr. James A. Henshall.

Author of the 1881 *Book of the Black Bass*, Henshall was a medical doctor and passionate bass angler. The most quoted line in bass fishing literature belongs to him: "I consider him (black bass), inch for inch and pound for pound, the gamest fish that swims."

Henshall's passion, said Long, was to promote black bass as "a pre-eminent gamefish." The doctor, however, was also a "lumper," countering decades of science that preceded him.

Long coined that phrase as the opposite to "splitters," which describes those who recognize multiple bass species.

"Henshall did a lot of really good work, but he considered the spotted bass a smallmouth, the Guadalupe a largemouth, and the

Florida a largemouth," Long explained, "and he was the authoritative voice."

So, even though the smallmouth bass and then largemouth bass were identified in 1802, the spotted bass in 1819, the Florida bass in 1822, and the Guadalupe bass in 1874, Henshall's lumping successfully countered their acknowledgement as separate species until the 1940s.

By the way, no one knows where that first smallmouth was caught before it was shipped to France to be analyzed and given its Latin name. But what Long discovered is that the black bass's keystone designation as *Micropterus* was based on a damaged dorsal fin. "It looked like it had a second, smaller dorsal," he said. "And that word means small fin or wing."

With improvement in science over the decades, especially in genetics, Henshall's lumping has fallen out of favor, and we're not likely to name any new species based on an imperfection. Also, we've become much more selective about how and when we stock. In order to sustain fisheries we're focused on improving habitat as never before.

All those are good things. Seeing what has happened in New York, though, I'm troubled by our politicians and their propensity for repeating harmful chapters in our history.

Dogs are among the best fishing buddies.

A New Fishing Buddy

My most loyal fishing friend died last spring.

Although she didn't care anything about fish or even fishing, she always was eager to go with me. She didn't complain about getting up early or staying late. She loved swimming and chasing muskrats, but, somehow she knew not to give in to temptation when I carried a rod and reel as we walked along the shore of the lake behind my house.

I'll never forget the vision of her lying on the dock beside my Little Brother Jesse, her head on his chest, as they shared the sleep of the innocent.

Early on, though, I realized Ursa the Devil Dog was no pushover. One night, we left her on shore as we paddled out for some night fishing. We made that mistake only once. That's all it takes to realize that wrestling a wet and wriggling, 70-pound Lab mix into a john boat in the dark is a comedic catastrophe.

When I was a child, my family always had dogs, and some of them went fishing with me from time to time, but they were pets. At the lake they were more of a nuisance than anything else, especially if we were using raw bacon as bait.

Ursa was my first canine companion. In addition to going fishing with me, she joined me on walks every morning. She visited friends and ran errands with me. With her unconditional love and affection, she cheered me when I was sad and calmed me when I was angry.

But she refused to chase a Frisbee. Yeah, she'd humor me and catch it if I threw the Frisbee directly to her, and she'd bring it to me. But chase it? No way. As with refusing to be left on shore, her disdain for "fetch" helped me appreciate her individuality and recognize her devotion to being my fishing buddy as a rare gift.

With the first anniversary of her death fast approaching, I decided I was finally ready for another canine fishing friend. My original idea was to get a pup, or at least a dog no more than 6 months old. However, when I visited the pet adoption center today, I discovered only adult dogs were available. Disappointed, I decided to look at the animals anyway.

Seeing all those dogs in cages—barking, whining for affection, or cowering in the corners, made me want to cry. I've visited animal shelters before, but not since Ursa became my companion more than fourteen years earlier. Our relationship had changed me in a way I hadn't realized, and I suddenly understood that many of these affection-starved dogs would never have a chance to enrich a human life the way Ursa had mine.

I knew the animal's age was no longer a priority for me. I studied them all, petted as many as possible, and finally decided I wanted to adopt a black female about 2 years old. She was the only one left from a litter of pups brought to the shelter. In other words, she'd lived there almost her entire life. She's a mix of some kind, possibly greyhound and Lab, or greyhound and collie.

I took her outside for a walk in the cold, winter sunshine. She didn't seem much interested in exercise, but preferred to sit and lean against my leg. I gently stroked her head. I told her what a good girl she was.

And I recognized the beginning of a spirit-renewing companionship we've both been deprived of for too long. I think Ursa would approve.

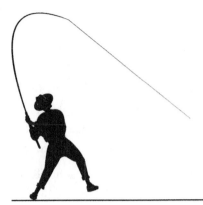

Faith and Fishing
By Teeg Stouffer

(Teeg Stouffer is the founder and executive director of Recycled Fish, an organization that encourages conservation through stewardship.)

*F*or me, fishing is a matter of faith.

Fishing is in my DNA. I was *made* this way. I come from a fishing family, so I had exposure to water all my life, but my folks say that as soon as I could walk they had to be careful with me around water. If they so much as looked away, I'd toddle right into it.

In the fourth grade we were given an assignment to write a letter to our heroes. Other kids wrote to actor Kirk Cameron or Joe "Refrigerator" Perry from the Chicago Bears. I wrote to Jimmy Houston. I was the only kid in the class who got a letter back— along with an 8x10 glossy of Jimmy holding two giant Okeechobee largemouth bass.

Another thing about me is that I've always liked to talk. That's pretty consistent with most fishermen I know: we are storytellers. (I'm aware that in some circles, the term "storyteller" is a five-dollar-word that means "liar.")

When I was 14 years old I had my first radio show. By the time I was 16, I worked at WHO-Radio, the Midwestern talk radio powerhouse that launched Ronald Reagan's career. (My joke after mentioning that is, "Hey, who knows where I could wind up?")

When college rolled around for me, I was recruited by a small college in Forest City, Iowa—Waldorf—where they planned to do something revolutionary. They were going to start the country's first all-digital, student-run radio station, multimedia lab, and television studio. Every student at the school would get a laptop, which was almost unheard of back then. This was one of the pilot schools for IBM's Laptop University program. Plus, I'd be able to get my BA in just three years, and complete part of my studies in England, at Oxford. Not only that, they wanted to give me a *full ride scholarship*.

I took it.

Waldorf is also a Lutheran college, so I had to take religion classes.

Now, bear this in mind, before going to college I'd never heard the gospel. My understanding about church-and-stuff was that "God is good, but church is bad." My understanding of who God was, and what He was all about, seemed fuzzy.

At Waldorf, we had no choice about religion classes. That meant I read the *Bible* for the first time, and I heard the gospel. Plus, the radio station I was there to help start played only Christian music, but those religion classes and all those cheesy Christian songs aren't what made me a Christian.

What made me a Christian was my relationship with one professor, Mark Newcom. The way I saw it, he had challenges in life that most folks don't, and he handled them—and handled life—with such grace, energy, sincerity, and love . . . that I thought, *whatever this guy's got, I want it.*

And what he had that I didn't was a relationship with Jesus. So, I jumped in. I started following Christ.

After college I landed a radio job down in Springfield, Missouri. I started out as the promotions director for an alternative radio station, but by the time I left I was marketing director for a five-station Clear Channel group. Along the way I married Amy, the editor of the

Waldorf college yearbook, a newspaper girl who got an early jump on her career, too. She became a TV producer in Springfield. We were a media couple and we got awards and other stuff.

I don't know if you know anyone who works in the media, and I don't want to paint with too broad a brush, but I'll tell you that, generally speaking, you can either have a successful career in the media or a successful marriage. Having both is darned hard. We decided to opt for the successful marriage, so we quit our media jobs, sold our house and all our belongings, and packed life down to three suitcases. We took our two dogs and three suitcases and started traveling all over America, doing promotional tours and executing large-scale events. Think of us as the people who drive the Oscar Meyer Weiner Mobile. Although we never did that tour, specifically, we did stuff like that. We lived in hotels in new towns every week. We got to have amazing outdoor adventures all across North America when we weren't working, and we met interesting people, as you might imagine, traveling full time like modern-day nomads.

Our travels took us through Colorado. I bought a fly rod, and it became an extension of me on the Gunnison River. I haven't put it down since.

After a couple of years living in hotels, Amy was ready to "nest," so we decided to settle down in either Austin, Denver, or Seattle. The very week we made up our minds to do that, three things fell into place all at once that made us think that God was leading us to the Seattle area.

So, we moved there.

That's what landed me in the Cascade Mountains on one amazing day, when everything fell into place. I bet you've had days like this. Athletes call it "being in the zone." It's that moment when everything falls into place—when everything fits together.

I was fishing on a stream that had once borne salmon, but now doesn't. The stream still has lots of trout, even if they get their start in hatcheries. On this day, everywhere I thought a fish might live, it did. Every cast I made landed where I wanted it to, and just about every time my fly floated into the slot where a fish ought to be, one rose. I hooked it, landed it, and set it free.

After such an amazing day, I sat down for a time of prayer. Even the light was perfect— golden light dancing on the rocks and across water that sung its way downstream.

In that moment, I had the most gut-wrenching sense of loss. I felt that if I ever had kids, what I was experiencing right then was something they wouldn't know. That it would all be gone, like the salmon. It seemed that what I was feeling on the riverbank, high in the mountains, was fleeting—and we would lose it because of how we are as humans.

I groaned a simple prayer, "Lord, don't let us lose this!"

And in that holy moment, in my spirit, I felt as if God said, "Then do something about it." All these experiences—all these things I told you about—having seen the whole country and been wired as a communicator and an event-maker and a marketer, having had fishing in my DNA and having been given these advantages and opportunities—I saw all that come together in a single moment.

So I took that word as a calling, as a prayer answered, and as a mission: *to do something about it.*

So I started this non-profit organization called Recycled Fish.

Six months in, I wanted out. All the books about starting non-profit organizations say, "at this point, consult your lawyer." Amy and I didn't know any lawyers and we didn't have any money to hire one. So I hit my knees in the middle of our little apartment in Puyallup, Washington, and said, "Lord, if you want me to do this, I'm gonna need some help." The next day, my phone rang and—no joke—we got pro bono representation from one of the biggest law firms in the country. Every time we've come to a tough spot with the cause, God has done something incredible to get us past it. So I figure I'm doing what I ought to be doing.

Today, Recycled Fish is a national, grassroots 501 (c) 3 non-profit organization with stewards in all 50 states and 20 countries. Something like 15,000 men and women have taken the Sportsman's Stewardship Pledge and agreed to be caretakers of their local waters through everyday living. The educational organization helps build on the catch-and-release ethic. What motivates us to let 'em swim—knowing it'll help us catch more and bigger fish today and leave strong fisheries for coming generations—can also motivate us to change the way we take care of our lawns, to recycle, and to put in a low flow showerhead. Stuff like that matters just as much as what we do on the water, because our lifestyle runs downstream.

For me, picking up trash at the lake or dog poop in my back yard isn't just a nice thing to do for our waters, it's an act of worship. Not "green living," but Creation Care.

You see, when I'm outside, I connect with not just Creation, but the Creator. God said, "I won't live in a house built with man's hands." Now what He meant was that He wants to live in each of us, that we get to be His dwelling place, but I figure there's also a little bit of Him not wanting to get cooped up in some building. It's easier for me to get connected with Him when I'm outside the trappings of man's hands. Outside the confines of a building. Outside the imprisonment of religion, which can smother and stifle and steal the freedom that Jesus showed up to bring us.

God uses many images of nature to describe His Nature in the *Bible*. In fact, I think all of Creation reflects its Creator. Early on, God entrusted it to us. He said, "I'll take care of Heaven, you take care of Earth," and in the thousands of years since, we've done a terrible job of holding up our end of that deal.

But something happens in our wiring when that inanimate graphite rod in our hands springs to life, connected to another living thing. Think about this: why would it be fun to catch a fish? And why is it even more fun to watch a big fish swim away? Who knows, but it is. Logic cannot define it. There's no reasoning to it, no explanation for someone who hasn't experienced it. But it is fun. It's healing, being out there. It transcends a peace, and it's about more than neurons and psychology. That dancing rod touches something in our souls, and, if you ask me, something in our spirits as well.

Fishing uniquely connects us to nature. Hiking, kayaking, hunting, and golf—all these things get us outside, but fishing does something nothing else can. The tug is the drug. Studies prove it, and that connection with nature—with Creation—can help define a relationship with the Creator. With God. Jesus didn't show up here to bring us a bunch of rules. He came for the sake of relationship— relationships created, or renewed, or restored. Relationships rooted in all the right stuff, like truth and grace and love. Out there in the outdoors, whether it's alone, or with a family member or a buddy or a bunch of buddies, that's a sweet spot for relationship.

Take away the relationship, and taking care of nature is just more rules. Just some burdensome doctrine that gets to be about arguments and finger pointing. In a relationship with our water, and with the One who *made the waters,* our opportunity to care for this great place takes on new meaning.

In the eco-movement there are folks who believe in taking care of nature for nature's sake. People are viewed as parasites; we're in the way of nature, we're to blame for what's gone wrong, and if we'd get out of the way—if we'd go away—nature would be okay.

But that's not God's view at all. The pinnacle of Creation isn't mountains or oceans or stars in the cosmos. *It's us. We are his masterpiece. We are His best work.*

He made all this for us to enjoy with Him. He did all this because of His love for us. He made the mountains and the oceans and the stars and the cosmos so we could share it together.

That's a different deal altogether. We're not in the way of Creation; we are Created in His image as His best work. Because all this, Creation is made to be a source of our provision, and when we take care of it, we take care of one another. We also take care of "the least of these," the people who are most affected when the environment is imperiled.

So when I'm out there on the stream, make no mistake about it, I want to pick the right bait, lure, or fly and offer it with the right presentation, and I want to fish it in the right spot at the right time so I'll catch more and bigger fish, but that's just the superficial part.

There's a supernatural part, too, something happening beyond the confines of nature. An exchange between me and the One who dreamed up me and the stream in the first place, before I was a good idea hatched between my mom and my dad, before the first drops of water that make that stream fell from the sky.

That's why I know I'm not alone when I say, that for me, *fishing is a matter of faith*.

Bad days of fishing don't exist, no matter how slow the bite.

A Bad Day While Fishing

I honestly can say I've never had a bad day of fishing, and I suspect that most who love the sport would agree. That is not to say I haven't had a bad day *while* fishing. The distinction is subtle, but significant.

A poor bite and/or miserable weather might temper my enthusiasm in describing a day on the water, but I'd still rather be there than most anyplace else. Whether the fish are biting or have lockjaw, whether the skies are sunny or gray, fishing still is fishing.

That isn't to say embarrassing and/or painful things have not occurred during my pursuit of bass, bluegill, trout, and a host of other species. They have, but they were the result of mistakes on my part or human frailties beyond my control—not uncooperative fish or weather.

The first I can remember occurred when I was 10 or 11 years old and fishing alone for bluegill from shore. With my bait hanging about 6 feet below a bobber, I flung a sidearm cast and somehow, some way, the hook looped around in front of my face and pierced my lower eyelid.

The cast stopped abruptly and at first I didn't know what had happened. My fingers soon told me, as I found the worm-covered hook hanging just below my right eye.

On the positive side, I could find no blood and felt no pain. On the negative, I didn't have a knife to cut the line. Rod in my left hand and line draped around me, I walked up to the nearest road, not quite sure what to do after that. Fortunately, a man in a pickup stopped almost immediately and took me to the emergency room.

I later learned my parents had been told I was admitted to the hospital with blood streaming from my right eye. Actually, it was a blend of tears and worm juice. As it turned out, my eye wasn't damaged at all. Shots to my face to deaden the pain while the hook was extracted were the worst part, and even though I got to wear a cool eye patch for a couple of days, the entire ordeal certainly made for a bad day while fishing.

Another occurred when I managed to get my four-wheel-drive Bronco stuck in knee-deep mud and, in the days before cell phones, had to walk a couple of miles before I could call a tow truck. Then there was the time I fell overboard while reaching to net a friend's fish. Had it happened during summer, I might have enjoyed the unexpected dip, but during March, the water was icy and our day on the lake reached an abrupt end. Both of those were bad days while fishing as well.

Fortunately, I've never had bodily function emergencies during a day on the water, but I've been in the company of those who have. For some, a pleasant day of fishing quickly deteriorated into a bad day while fishing. Two of them picked the wrong places to go ashore and their private parts became bug buffets. Others found themselves suddenly spending more time relieving themselves than fishing because of digestive upset. Unfortunately, as we age, we are more and more likely to succumb to the latter, as well as bladder problems, while on the water. Medications, surgery, disease, transplants, all contribute to a loss of bladder and/or bowel control. For many of us, it becomes a myth that fishing is something we can enjoy all our lives.

Or does it? Anglers are nothing if not innovative when it comes to pursuing their passion, and that led Matt Smith to create the

Bassroom, a portable bathroom for a boat that can be set up and taken down in seconds.

Mostly, he was thinking about providing privacy when he came up with the idea, as well as guarding against illegal "over exposure" on public waters. "You never know who has a camera or video phone and would enjoy the 10 minutes of fame by posting a video of you 'caught in the act' on YouTube or similar social network websites," he told me.

Of course, the Bassroom is also more eco-friendly than you-know-what and saves an angler the time of motoring all the way back to the porta-potties at the launch site or a secluded stretch of shoreline.

But what Smith has learned is that many Bassroom buyers are aging Baby Boomers. His invention, they tell him, has allowed them to keep fishing or to start again, after being forced off the water by bladder or bowel problems that dictated quick access to a bathroom.

For many people, Matt Smith's Bassroom is the sole reason they can continue experiencing the joy of never having a bad day of fishing. That's because it eliminates one of the biggest causes of a bad day *while* fishing.

When lakefront property is returned to nature, it not only benefits fish. It also attracts wildlife, like this fawn the author saw one June morning.

Animal Magnetism

*M*y house sits on one and a half acres, with much of the land sloping steeply down to the lake. As soon as I moved in, I started allowing grass and weeds to grow unchecked on both sides.

My neighbors across the road soon noticed I wasn't mowing and diplomatically questioned me about it. They smiled when I explained that, as an angler, I knew leaving land to exist naturally would cut down on runoff and improve water quality, with the end result being better fishing.

The previous owners, they said, had dumped truckloads of topsoil on those slopes in hopes of turning them into manicured lawn. A couple of downpours washed most of the dirt into the lake.

I wasn't surprised. Ignorance about runoff pollution is one of the main reasons it remains such a threat to our rivers, streams, and oceans. Too many waterfront property owners cultivate their land right down to the water's edge, allowing soil, fertilizers and pesticides to be washed in by rainfall and snowmelt. Too many don't know, or choose to ignore, the basic premise that what goes on the land eventually gets into the water.

Call my actions self-serving if you like, but the fact is that anglers are among the nation's most ardent conservationists and everyone benefits from their devotion to clean up our waters and improve aquatic habitat.

And, as it turns out, wildlife benefits as well. By July of that first summer, I had watched skunks, possums, rabbits, and squirrels prowling about in the unmown grass just uphill from a stand of oaks that separates it from the lake. One drizzly morning I saw two young raccoons rooting about just outside my dining room window. Then, in August, I enjoyed the antics of a turkey hen and her chicks as they alternated between bathing in the dirt along the road and chasing grasshoppers in the grass.

The following June, I walked out early one morning to see a spotted fawn nestled in the grass, not 30 feet from my basement door. The young deer continued sleeping as I ran back inside, grabbed my camera, and returned to take photos.

The next summer, I walked out at sunrise one morning to come face to face with a young black bear. I did *not* photograph it. I bolted one way and it the other, but that wasn't my scariest moment. That occurred when I looked out my front door one evening to see the full, fluffy tail of a long-haired cat just as it slipped off the porch to prowl among the shrubs. I keep a feeder nearby and immediately suspected it was after birds. My first impulse was to open the door and go charging after the intruder to frighten it away. Fortunately, I paused—just long enough to see the "cat" bounce back onto the porch. My brief hesitation saved me from a healthy dose of "eau de skunk," of that I have no doubt.

Yeah, the natural habitat, along with proximity to the lake, does encourage wildlife to come a little closer to the house. Every spring, a black snake or two curls up on the tops of those same shrubs to enjoy the midday sun. Occasionally, a speckled king snake sublets.

One morning, I lifted my outdoor thermometer to get the key that hangs under it. Incredibly, a baby bat about the size of that key was hanging behind it. Every year since, a single bat has made the underside of my deck its summer home. Of course, I don't know if the bat that stayed there last summer was the same as the one I found under the thermometer, or even the same as the year before, but some kind of link must exist that keeps the tradition going.

Over the years, Mother Nature has helped me improve my little wildlife paradise. Fierce winds took the top out of an oak tree and it toppled perfectly onto the shoreline and into the lake shallows. The submerged branches allow alga growth, which attracts small fish. They, in turn, draw predators, including bass and birds such as kingfishers and little green herons. Meanwhile, turtles use the branches that remain above water to sunbathe.

I've used other branches felled by winds and ice storms to make brushpiles, where birds and other small animals can take refuge at night and during winter.

I could go on and on about all the critters I've seen in that brush and along the lake's shoreline, as well as in the grass and wildflowers. But I'm going to skip to today.

I keep a path mowed so I can walk through the grassy area without being assaulted by chiggers and ticks. Animals, especially deer, use the path as well. Just before sunset during winter, I often see three or four does and yearlings pass by.

This morning I looked out to see a young fox dart along the path and then spring into the grass. I suspected it was hunting, but then it bounced back out and ran, with another fox hot on its heels. For 15 minutes I watched those two gambol about like puppies. They chased, and pounced, and reared up at each other in mock assaults.

I thought about grabbing my camera for some photos, but to do that, I would have had to walk away from that rare and beautiful sight for a few seconds. I couldn't do it.

My conclusion: people who have the option of allowing a little of their property to return to nature and don't do it are missing out. It's good for the land and water, it's good for the fish and wildlife, and it's good for keeping us connected to all of those, which enriches us in ways we can't imagine unless we experience them.

The value of fishing cannot be measured in terms of dollars.

What It's Really Worth

*F*ishery leaders have long known that successful advocacy depends on economic justification. They recognize that recreational fishing's worth must be proven by the numbers to state and federal decision-makers who authorize and appropriate funds for fisheries and conservation programs.

I understand and support that strategy. Recreational fishing generates more than $125 billion annually in economic output, plus more than 1 million jobs. This is clearly worth the money we invest, and that's something politicians understand.

But you and I both know that angling's intrinsic value is what keeps us going to the lakes, rivers, and oceans. We fish for fun, to relax, to compete, and to spend quality time with friends and family. We fish to forget—and we fish to remember. We fish to lower our blood pressure and we fish to raise our adrenaline.

Did you know, though, that fishing is also magic? That probably doesn't mean much to the politicians who control the purse strings, but parents and volunteers will tell you fishing works in ways we can't quantify to enrich the lives of millions who endure illness, injury, and disabilities. As much as we might think angling means to us, both economically and inherently, it can mean even more to people who are hurting.

"Fishing and other outdoor activities are a diversion from the reality of life-threatening illnesses," says Gene Gilliland, a B.A.S.S. member who helps organize an annual day on the water for children with chronic and life-threatening illnesses at Camp Cavett on Lake Texoma.

"This gives them a chance to be kids again. It's amazing how fired up they get over going for a ride in the boat and fishing."

Gilliland especially remembers the mother of one of those children. Following camp the previous year, she said all her son talked about was fishing and riding in the bass boats.

"She went on and on about how he talked about catching sand bass and perch and going fast in the boat," Gene says. "She said he talked and talked about it ... right up to the day he died from cancer.

"The story grabbed at our hearts. But the mother assured us what we did that day at the lake made a difference in those kids' lives. That's what keeps us coming back, year after year."

Fishing makes a difference, too, for war veterans who've been wounded and are struggling to adjust to the new reality of their civilian lives. "We see the benefits over and over," reports Heroes on the Water, an organization that takes injured warriors fishing in kayaks. It adds, however, that "the rehabilitation aspect was an unintended consequence of helping injured service members."

Realization of that aspect of the magic occurred with a veteran suffering from traumatic brain injury. He stuttered, wouldn't talk, and wanted to be left alone. He had to be persuaded to get in a kayak for a four-hour outing.

"When we were helping him out, we asked how his morning was," a spokesman for Heroes says. "For 30 seconds, he was jabbering away, talking about how great kayaking was, how he caught five fish, and how he really enjoyed the time on the water.

"Then he—and we—realized he was talking normally."

For the first time in two years.

The stuttering eventually returned, but the soldier said, 'Now I know I can do it (speak normally). Now I have hope."

Fishing and other outdoor activities provide hope for children with autism as well.

"What I've discovered about people on the (autism) spectrum is that they're highly institutionalized," says Anthony Larson, father of a 6-year-old with the disability and owner of Coulee Region Adventures, which takes special needs children into the outdoors.

An institutional lifestyle, he theorizes, puts to "sleep" the part of the brain that makes maps and encourages creativity. Additionally, those on the spectrum often have issues with their body placement, as well as linking their bodies with emotions and estimating where they are in time and space.

"So, when children participate in the outdoors, they're using parts of the brain that normally don't get used, as well as using under-used muscle groups for balance, climbing, depth perception, and distance estimates—the simple survival mechanisms we take for granted."

Freedom is another benefit. "When I have my son or any others outdoors, they are not spectrum kids," Larson says. "They've normal, and the same rules apply to them that apply to us.

"I recently took a group of special needs adolescents on a hunting trip. We had 10 kids and 15 adults. We just let the kids run. Great thing is, we had zero incidents. Everyone got along, everyone reminded each other to take their meds when it was time, and everyone had fun. They all took pride in being part of the camp and getting involved with their environment."

A final benefit is exhaustion, Larson emphasizes. "It's a lot of work to be outdoors. Like I tell my son's therapists, he can't fight if he's tired."

Eli Delany also noted the therapeutic value of fishing for his son, and that prompted him to found My Little Buddy's Boat, an autism awareness program now promoted by many of the top professional anglers.

"Communication between a parent and a child with autism doesn't come easy," Delany says. "But Luke loves the water. He's really starting to enjoy the fishing part of it, casting his rod and holding the bass after we catch them. And he likes to look at the birds.

"His favorite thing is to say, 'Go fast!' For him, that just means getting the boat up on plane, but there's such a gleam in his eye when he says it. Being out there together is a great connection for us."

And Katie Gage, a California mother of two sons with autism, adds this: "Fishing has proven to be great therapy. They can find peace on the water, and they connect with their love of science and nature and stewardship. No pressure, just fish!"

So ... you can tell the politicians that angling is worth more than $125 billion annually if you want to. I say it's priceless.

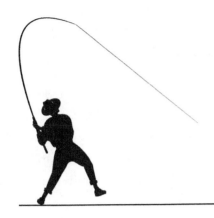

9/11

*M*exico's Lake El Salto was hot. In a fall of 2000 trip to Angler's Inn, a friend and I had caught and released 13 bass of 10 pounds or more, with the largest a hefty 13 pounds, 8 ounces. We didn't even count all the 8- and 9-pounders we boated.

With that in mind, four of us planned to go there in October of 2001, hoping to enjoy similar action. But then religious fanatics hijacked four planes, took down the World Trade Center twin towers, and killed 2,996 people on September 11, 2001.

My friend Norm and I decided to go fishing anyway, but two of our party backed out. I'm not certain if they were fearful of being hijacked or just didn't want to deal with the wartime-status security we'd encounter at the airports. Whatever their reasons, most of those who'd booked a trip to Angler's Inn during that week also decided not to go. That meant fewer than a dozen of us were at a resort that could accommodate 45 to 50.

With such a small group, this meant we could get to know everyone, especially in the evenings. Those were the times we'd sit out under the thatched-roof palapas, drinking margaritas before dinner. Normally, we shared stories about the day's fishing, with lots of laughing and teasing lightening the mood. But on our first evening there the mood was somber. Not sad exactly, but more reserved than usual. I don't remember how the conversation started or what we talked about at first, but eventually we learned that several of our small group were from one family.

"We come here every year," the father said. "We almost didn't come this time. Our son was killed on 9/11."

From my point of view, time stopped, as did the rocking chairs some of us were sitting in. Here we were, a couple of thousand miles from New York City, and we were in the presence of a family freshly grieving because of the World Trade Center tragedy.

"But he loved this place," the father continued. "So we talked about it and decided we should come. He would want us to."

In a cruel twist, their son didn't work in either of the towers. He didn't even live in New York City. He was just there in an adjoining building, because of the travel his job required. They said that debris from an explosion flew through a window and struck him a fatal blow to the head. I don't remember anything about our conversation after that, but I'll never forget those few minutes when this family spoke so courageously of their loss and so lovingly of how their son loved to fish and how they were honoring him by being there.

Fishing, even fishing at a world-class resort such as Angler's Inn on Lake Salto, doesn't cure cancer. It doesn't destroy depression or heal illness and disease. However, revelations of the joy that it bestows — even in the aftermath of 9/11 — does remind us of what's important as we live out our too-short years on this planet.

I was reminded of that recently when a friend died following a long illness. She introduced me to El Salto, and we often fished there together. Outside the pros, she was the best worm fisherman I ever met. She said it was because she sat down and took her time; too many people, she said, fish too fast.

Whatever the reason, Katie Watson was legendary at El Salto for the many big bass she caught. Then a painful disease prevented her from going to the lake, but when I'd call her, we'd plan our next trip. Did either of us really believe it would happen? I don't know.

What I do know is that we'd talk about all the fun we had on previous trips, and I could hear in her voice the pleasure those memories gave her, even as her body was wracked by pain.

Were memories helping ease the pain for the family I met in October of 2001? Did being at Lake El Salto just days after their son was killed enhance those memories for them?

I hope so. I believe so. I believe so because time spent fishing is an investment that never depreciates. It's always there in our memory banks, ready for a quick withdrawal and infusion to help sustain us, even in the wake of tragedies such as 9/11.

Bluegills and bullheads hook us when we are young anglers.

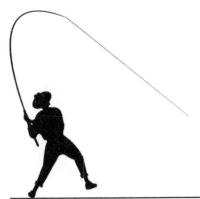

Waiting for a Bite

When I was young, I couldn't bear the thought of being on the shore of a lake, river, or ocean without a rod in my hands. Water was there to be fished. Period.

I often expressed wonder that people could go camping—or even worse—boating without intending to fish. *I mean, what's the point? I remember thinking. What are they going to do? Won't they get bored? Don't they know what they're missing?*

When my family went on vacation to Florida, my parents and siblings would go to the beach; I'd go fishing at the closest pier or causeway. When we visited relatives in South Texas, I'd coax my uncle to take me "surf" fishing. Actually, he didn't need much coaxing, and, looking back, I realize how kind and patient he was with me. He showed not a hint of anger or frustration when I dropped his spinning gear in the sand so I could use both hands to grasp my first saltwater fish—a skipjack herring.

Now, with the wisdom of age, I realize that "catching" was secondary. What I lived for was wetting a line, with the *hope* of catching fish. What *might be* was more important than what *was*, notwithstanding the joy I felt as I clasped the slimy skipjack against my chest.

So I fished and fished and fished, as much as I possibly could, with my passion stoked by an unquenchable thirst for knowledge that would improve my odds and heighten my hope. Understandably, I spent lots of time *not* catching fish as I figured out what worked and what did not:

Catfish don't bite much during the day, unless they're bullheads.

To catch bluegill, cover the hook with the worm and don't leave much hanging free.

A spincast rod and reel are no good for throwing popping bugs—unless you use about 18 inches of line to tie the bug to the tail of a topwater bait.

A flounder can straighten the hook on a doll fly intended for crappie.

Don't stay in the same spot too long if the fish aren't biting.

Don't leave a rod unattended, especially when fishing from a pier high above the water.

Put an overhand knot at the end of the line before tying a cinch knot to keep it from slipping.

With all of that slow time, I also began taking note of what was going on in the natural world around me. I still remember watching what I thought was a pterodactyl fly overhead. Later, I saw a big, gawky bird stalking and spearing fish with its laser beak just down the shore from me, and I made the connection. Eventually I learned its name: great blue heron.

I'll never forget looking down at a bush near me and seeing what I swear was a giant green spider that looked as if it should be from another world—and was possibly capable of consuming human children. Was it really there? Probably not. But I took off like a rocket without a second glance. And when I finally had bolstered my courage enough to return the next day, it was gone.

As I spent more time waiting for bullheads and bluegills to bite, I learned the great blue heron isn't the only fish-eating, wading bird. I discovered that a frog isn't a frog. It's a bullfrog or a cricket frog or a leopard frog. Before it's any of those, it's a tadpole, and before that, it's an egg in a jellylike mass.

Also a turtle isn't just a turtle. It's a snapper, a softshell, or a slider, with the former seeming to have both a nastier disposition and a longer neck than its cousins. A crawdad, no matter how big, is incapable of amputating your finger. But it still hurts. Red berries are pretty, but some of them are attached to poison ivy.

I educated myself about raptors after a great horned owl swooped down on my Jitterbug. One summer day, I noted that not all dragonflies are the same and some aren't even dragonflies; they're damselflies, which rest with their wings upright and parallel to their bodies, instead of horizontal.

I slowly recognized how light and wind can play on the tendrils of a blossom, creating an optical illusion. Was that what I mistook for a giant green spider? Probably, but to this day I'm not certain. Possibly it *was* an alien arachnid.

Whatever it was, I learned to appreciate all the wonders around me. In turn, that appreciation fostered in me a desire to educate myself about not only what I saw, but what I hoped to see. From familiarity with individual species, I advanced to how they relate to one other and how they fit together in ecosystems.

I thought about this recently when I walked down to the lake behind my house—without a fishing rod. As the sun set, I built a fire and sat back to enjoy a cool spring day's transition into night. I smiled as I remembered my youthful intolerance for those who would deign to go camping or boating without fishing gear.

I watched bats and fireflies, listened to cricket frogs and whippoorwills, and realized how different it was for me now. All of those hours waiting for bites gave me time to open my eyes and see what was going on around me in nature's classroom. They led me to recognize birds, reptiles, and mammals of all kinds and derive pleasure simply from observing their behavior. They gave me time to watch the wind, appreciate the clouds, and study the stars. Over time, this enjoyment of nature, given to me by reluctant fish, has become a pastime I do not need a fishing rod to enjoy—even when I'm on the water.

Oh, I still love to fish. I still get excited planning the next trip, and most of the time when I'm near water, I have a fishing rod in my hands. With age and experience, however, I've realized that the pleasure to be derived from fishing comes from more than just a bite at the end of the line.

Go Fishing and Find Out

A friend once told me that when his father was criticized by his non-hunting friends about his fondness for fishing and hunting, he responded that his pursuits had "much more of an ecological integrity and a biological and cultural basis than their golfing or even attendance at professional sporting events."

Those wise words have led me to the realization that fishing is equally important as a means as it is an end. Yes, fishing is synonymous with relaxation, catching fish, having fun, and spending time with friends and family. Those are all valuable "ends" that make life better.

Fishing is also the means by which we connect with both our humanity and nature as we pursue those ends. In the outdoors, only hunting and possibly farming are comparable. Sure, all athletic sports are healthful pastimes, but none of them transport us so completely into the web of life as fishing and hunting. We might no longer fish or hunt to feed our families, but these pastimes takes us closer to what life is all about than anything else I can think of—except for maybe getting lost in the wilderness or being pursued by a grizzly bear.

And in getting closer to what life is all about, we implicitly recognize our place in it and, as a consequence, are healthier and happier in our everyday existence.

What is life all about? Go fishing and find out.

We must make it our mission to share fishing.

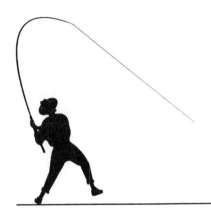

In the End . . .

*O*ne of my first assignments as a young sports writer was to interview an 85-year-old man who bicycled daily.

I don't remember much about that interview except what he told me at the end. "People don't use their legs enough," he said. "One of these days, they won't even have them anymore."

Now, the obesity epidemic that has occurred in recent years does give me pause, but I'm still not ready to buy into the idea that our legs will devolve into worthless stumps. Rather, I remember what he said because it's provocative. Over the years, his words have often inspired me to look at many aspects of modern life with a new perspective and to wonder what lies ahead.

That brings me to consideration of what the future holds for recreational fishing. What began as means of gathering food to survive thousands of years ago has evolved into a pastime enjoyed today by an estimated 60 million people in this country and probably more than 100 million worldwide.

Yes, some of us still fish for food, but many of us have also recognized countless other reasons that keep us returning to the water with rods in our hands. We fish to spend time with family and friends. We fish to relax. We fish to compete. We fish to enjoy nature. We fish to remember. We fish to forget. We fish because—along with our families, our religions, and our jobs—fishing completes us.

But will it always? Or will something replace it?

Technology already tempts people to stay home instead of venturing into the world. Cell phones, computers and their associated offspring make face-to-face communication a threatened art, even as they encourage instant gratification. People live vicariously through an ever-growing number of television "reality" shows that bear little resemblance to real life. Video games grow continuously more realistic.

Put them altogether and what do you get? Virtual reality.

It's entirely reasonable to believe that one day you'll be able to go fishing any place in the world without leaving the comfy confines of your living room. You will select the season, the time of day, and the weather you'd like to experience. You will choose your gear with the press of a button or the flick of a cursor. As you kick back in your recliner, you will "feel" what it's like to ride in the boat, make a cast, and catch a fish.

You'll be able to catch as many fish as you'd like. And they can be as large you'd like too. Want a world record bass? No problem.

Compared to what it would normally cost you to fish the Amazon for peacocks, Lake Fork for largemouths, or the rivers of Argentina for trout, expenses would be minimal. You won't pay for an actual fishing trip; you'll pay for its realistic equivalent.

Sounds like utopia, right?

Not for me. What I treasure as much as anything about fishing is its unpredictability. Yeah, I know. You will probably be able to program that into your virtual reality experience as well.

But what about the pleasure of planning and preparing for the trip? Want to virtualize putting new line on your reels? How about sharpening hooks or tying flies?

And does programming unpredictability for the day's fishing really make it unpredictable? Can it adequately replace what you experience at dawn, when you stand in the bow scanning the shoreline to decide where you will place your topwater with the first cast of the day? Or can it duplicate what you feel as you stand hip deep in icy water, watching your dry fly drift into the sweet spot as the setting sun burns the sky crimson?

For me, it cannot. For most anglers, I believe, it cannot. The rush, the exhilaration, can come only from being in a real place during real time. For those who are yet to come, I don't know.

I still don't think we're going to lose our legs as my elderly bicycling friend predicted many years ago.

But I am fearful that we'll lose recreational fishing unless we make it our mission to share fishing as it really exists, with our children and our grandchildren ... unless we take them to the water and open their eyes to all of the many reasons we fish—and all reasons they should too.

Life is richer because of friends made while fishing.
Golfing great Johnny Miller (left) and Bruce Holt of G. Loomis
fished with the author for steelhead in Washington.

Acknowledgements

*M*y life has been made immeasurably richer by the many friends I've made while or because of fishing. This book is dedicated to them.

Sadly, listing them all would require another book, but their ranks include Dave Burkhardt, Norm Klayman, Bruce Holt, Jay Kumar, Troy Gibson, Billy Chapman, Todd Staley, Stephen Headrick, Carl Wengenroth, John Killian, Bill Frazier, Phil Morlock, David Ewald, Matt Smith, Chris Bennett, Gene Gilliland, Tim Cook, Bob DiStefano, Leonard Sonnenschein, and Sid Montgomery.

Additionally, I'd like to acknowledge the valuable contributions made by Dave Precht, Ken Cook, Bill Dance, Teeg Stouffer, Ben Leal, TChad Montgomery, Steve Chaconas, Kathy Magers, Bruce Condello, and Ross Gordon.

Author Robert Montgomery with a barramundi,
one of Australia's most popular game fish.
Photo by Dave Burkhardt

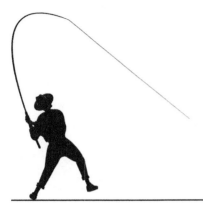

About the Author

*R*obert U. Montgomery has been hooked since he first went fishing on a Cub Scouts outing. His degree in journalism from the University of Missouri helped him turn his passion into a career as a fishing writer. He is author of Better Bass Fishing (Countryman Press) and founder of Activist Angler, a website devoted to promoting and protecting recreational fishing. He is a long-time Senior Writer specializing in conservation for B.A.S.S. Publications, and a Contributing Writer for Fishing Tackle Retailer Magazine.

In addition, the Missouri native is winner of the prestigious Homer Circle Fishing Communicator Award. He serves on the Board of Directors of Recycled Fish, a national conservation organization, and on the Conservation Pro Staff of Vanishing Paradise, a National Wildlife Federation initiative to restore Louisiana's fish and waterfowl habitat by reconnecting the Mississippi River it the state's wetlands.

He has fished in Africa, South America, Central America, and throughout much of North America and enjoys catching bluegill and crappie just as much as tarpon and sailfish. Well . . . nearly as much.

He has caught --- and released --- more than a dozen 10-pound largemouth bass.

Montgomery lives on a small lake in the eastern Ozarks with his dog, Pippa.

Printed in Great Britain
by Amazon

87145211R00129